Challenges of Global Enterprises

Kayoko Shiomi   Kazumi Tsutada   Angus McGregor

KINSEIDO

Kinseido Publishing Co., Ltd.
3-21 Kanda Jimbo-cho, Chiyoda-ku,
Tokyo 101-0051, Japan
Copyright © 2019 by   Kayoko Shiomi
                     Kazumi Tsutada
                     Angus McGregor

All rights reserved. No part of this publication may be reproduced, stored in a retrieval system, or transmitted, in any form or by any means, electronic, mechanical, photocopying, recording or otherwise, without the prior permission of the publisher.

First published 2019 by Kinseido Publishing Co., Ltd.

Cover design   Takayuki Minegishi
Text design / Editorial support   C-leps Co., Ltd.

Photos
p. 1 © Viorel Dudau | Dreamstime.com, p. 7 © Mohamed Ahmed Soliman | Dreamstime.com, p. 13 © Wellesenterprises | Dreamstime.com, p. 19 © Bragearonsen | Dreamstime.com, p. 37 © Alakoo | Dreamstime.com, p. 49 © Roman Tiraspolsky | Dreamstime.com, p. 55 © Calin Andrei Stan | Dreamstime.com, p. 61 © Alakoo | Dreamstime.com, p. 67 © Viorel Dudau | Dreamstime.com, p. 73 © Tupungato | Dreamstime.com

はじめに

　本書は、欧米や日本を含め、世界的に有名な企業や機関の取り組みと動向を、海外メディアを通じて紹介する。刻々と変化するグローバルビジネスにおいては、大企業であっても新しく起業した会社であっても、常に様々な課題を抱えながら挑戦を続けている。全ての試みや取り組みが成功するわけではない。かつては類を見ない規模で多角経営を行ってきた巨大企業であっても、時代の流れと共に衰退の道をたどるケースもある。本書では企業の成功例だけではなく、失敗例や直面する課題、新たに模索する方向性など、その光と影の部分についても焦点を当てる。

　取り扱うビジネス業種は、衣料、旅行、SNS、スポーツ用品、自動車、コーヒーショップ、ファストフード、Eコマース、エレクトロニクス、家具、IT、メガストア、エンターテイメントなど多岐にわたる。そのため、幅広いビジネス分野での最新の動向や、それに伴う課題なども把握することができる。

　英文記事は、アメリカやイギリスの有名な新聞や雑誌である *The Economist, The New York Times, The Guardian, Bloomberg, Financial Times, Business Insider* などから厳選しており、洗練されたオーセンティックな英語の文章に触れることができる。なお、難しいと思われる英語表現やビジネス用語は、Notes や Key Terms にて日本語訳や説明を記載している。

　本書を利用することにより、グローバル企業の動向や挑戦に関しての英文記事を興味深く読み、経済や経営に関する知見を広げると同時に、TOEIC などに頻出する単語やビジネス分野の語彙を、文脈の中で習得ができるようになることを願っている。

　最後に、本書を作成するにあたり、数々の助言をいただいた金星堂の西田碧氏と編集部の皆様に心より感謝申し上げたい。

編著者一同

本書の構成

本テキストは全 15 課からなり、各課は以下の構成になっている。

日本語導入文
各企業や機関の概要や取り組み、業種別の動向を日本語で説明している。

Before You Read
トピックに関する身近な質疑応答から、自分自身との関わりについて探る。

Vocabulary
英文記事に登場する重要語彙を、日本語訳とのマッチングで確認する。

Read the Article
800 語前後のオーセンティックな英文記事を読む。

Notes
難しいと思われる英単語や語句に、日本語訳や注釈をつけている。

Key Terms
ビジネス語彙や専門用語、固有名詞など、重要語句への補足説明をしている。

Grasp the Main Points
英文記事の全体的な内容に関して正誤問題を解き、内容把握をする。

Look for Specific Information
英文記事の詳細な情報に関して選択肢問題を解き、内容確認をする。

Find Further Information
英文記事から重要な情報を抜き出し、簡単にまとめる。

Dictation & Conversation Practice
会話の音声を聞いて空欄の穴埋めをした後、ペアで練習をする。

What Do You Think...?
英文記事と関連した、身近なトピックや社会的なテーマへの意見を出し合う。

なお、巻末には、各課に出てくる主要な語句を集めた Word List を掲載している。語彙の予習や復習、語彙の増強のために活用することができる。

Contents

01 Zara's Recipe for Success: More Data, Fewer Bosses 1

ファストファッションブランドの成功の鍵 — *Zara*

02 Airbnb's Challenge and New Direction 7

民泊ビジネスにおける課題と挑戦 — *Airbnb*

03 Augmented Reality Ecosystem in Facebook 13

拡張現実の構築で世界を変える？ — *Facebook*

04 Adidas Brings the Fast Shoe Revolution One Step Closer 19

「超高速」靴製造の技術革新 — *Adidas*

05 At Toyota, the Automation Is Human-Powered 25

自動車生産の自動化と職人技 — *Toyota*

06 How Starbucks Became a Successful Worldwide Brand 31

グローバルブランドの原点と成功への道のり — *Starbucks*

07 McDonald's Modern Marketing Methods 37

顧客に寄り添う新たなマーケティング戦略 — *McDonald's*

08 How TED Evolves and Where It Wants to Go Next 43

「広げる価値のあるアイデア」プレゼンの進化 — *TED*

09 Why Amazon Is the World's Most Innovative Company ········ 49

「最も革新的な企業」が目指す未来 — *Amazon*

10 Sony Comes Back from the Brink ········ 55

起死回生を賭けた取捨選択と新たな展望 — *Sony*

11 IKEA's New Business Move for Millennials ········ 61

若者の DIY 離れと新サービスの導入 — *IKEA*

12 How Google Has Changed the World ········ 67

検索エンジンが広げた世界のゆくえ — *Google*

13 How Did Walmart Get Cleaner Stores and Higher Sales? ········ 73

再生を賭けた経営戦略の転換 — *Walmart*

14 With Disney's Move to Streaming, a New Era Begins ········ 79

映像配信サービス新時代の到来 — *Disney*

15 How GE Went from American Icon to Astonishing Mess ········ 85

栄光と転落、暗中模索が続く巨大企業 — *General Electric*

巻末資料　Word List　········ 91

"In the end, what we offer our customer is fashion, and there's a human element to that."

Zara's Recipe for Success: More Data, Fewer Bosses
ファストファッションブランドの成功の鍵

カジュアルな洋服が安価で買えることから今や世界中で人気を集めているファストファッション。Zara、GAPやH&M、UNIQLOなど、多くの衣料ブランドがグローバル市場での展開にしのぎを削っている。苦戦する企業もある中、スペインに本社があるZaraは独自の戦略で業績を伸ばしている。他社に類を見ないその成功の鍵は一体、どこにあるのか。

Before You Read

トピックに関する次の質問に答えましょう。

1. Where do you usually buy clothes? Do you buy clothes at retailers that specialize in fast fashion? Explain why.
2. How often do you buy clothes and how much money do you spend on clothes?

Vocabulary

単語の日本語訳を選択肢より選び、その記号を記入しましょう。余分な選択肢が2つあります。

1. divine   (　)
2. retailer   (　)
3. struggle   (　)
4. revenue   (　)
5. surpass   (　)
6. flagship   (　)
7. replicate   (　)
8. prowess   (　)
9. reflect   (　)
10. release   (　)

a. 腕前、力量	d. 超える	g. 販売、公開	j. 努力・健闘する
b. 模倣する	e. 予算	h. 提案する	k. 最も重要な、主要な
c. 反映する	f. 小売業者	i. 推測する	l. 収益

Read the Article

1 Unlike rivals such as Gap, H&M, and Primark, Zara has no chief designer, and there's little discernible hierarchy. Its 350 designers are given unparalleled independence in approving products and campaigns, shipping fresh styles to stores twice a week. Guided by daily data feeds showing what's selling and what's stalling, the teams develop fashions for the coming weeks. Every morning, staff in Arteixo divine what's popular by monitoring sales figures and thousands of comments from customers, store managers, and country directors in cities as far-flung as Taipei, Moscow, and New York.

2 Zara's culture isn't as easily copied as the latest fashion trends, and that partly explains why Inditex, its parent company, is a breakaway success while most global clothing retailers are struggling. American Apparel filed for bankruptcy in November for a second time, sales have fallen at Gap stores, and profit is down at H&M. In contrast, Inditex powered ahead with an 11 percent rise in revenue in the first half of the year. "There isn't a magic formula," says Pablo Isla, Inditex's chairman and chief executive officer. "There are no stars. We are able to react to data during the season, but in the end, what we offer our customers is fashion, and there's a human element to that."

3 Controlled by Spanish billionaire Amancio Ortega, who this year briefly surpassed Bill Gates to become the world's richest man before falling back to second place, Inditex posted €20.9 billion ($22.2 billion) in sales last year, from 7,100 stores in 93 countries. Other Inditex brands such as Bershka, Massimo Dutti, and Pull & Bear are growing, but Zara still accounts for two-thirds of sales. Ortega hired Isla, a former Banco Popular Español executive, as CEO in 2005, but he hasn't retired. At 80, he still comes to work most days. Ortega remains one of the world's most secretive billionaires, leaving Isla to oversee Inditex.

4 One concern for Zara is managing its growth, says Andy Hughes, a retail analyst at UBS. With Inditex's sales almost doubling since 2009, Isla is adding stores at a slower pace, concentrating instead on a smaller number of flagship locations and its online business. Another concern is that rivals might figure out how to match Zara's quick turnarounds. "Everyone in the industry is trying to replicate its design prowess," Hughes says. "No one could match Inditex, but the gap might close."

5 Isla rejects the fast-fashion label for Zara, saying it doesn't reflect the time and detail that goes into designing each garment. And he says analysts place too much emphasis on Inditex's much-vaunted supply chain, a network of factories in Spain, Portugal, and Morocco that produces 60 percent of its merchandise. With production nearby, Inditex can quickly switch gears if weather or fashion trends change, getting designs into stores in as little as two or three weeks, while rivals' orders slowly make their way across the ocean on container ships.

6 Just as important is the way Inditex "pulls" ideas from consumers, Isla says, rather than designing collections months in advance and "pushing" goods on shoppers with ads. While analysts say H&M spends as much as 4 percent of sales on advertising, Inditex has virtually no ad budget apart from social media marketing. Since 2010, the data on what customers want has been augmented with information from online sales. Those are fueled by twice-weekly releases of new designs on Zara's website, highlighted with photos from rapid-fire shoots in Arteixo. On a rainy November day, buyers, analysts, and commercial managers sift through information on computers in a space the size of 22 football fields, engaging in a lively exchange of ideas with designers. "Without the design, there would be nothing," Isla says. "It's not a formula."

7 This means the designers are constantly tinkering. When military jackets turned out to be big sellers this autumn, the commercial team asked the designers to keep tweaking them with new fabrics and cuts. In May, a blue-and-white collarless women's coat for £69.99 (about $102 at the time) generated so much buzz that two fans created an Instagram account — @thatcoat — to document the craze. But instead of churning out more identical coats, design teams came up with different fabrics and prints using a similar cut, ranging in price from $69 to $189. "The root of Inditex's success is its predominantly short lead time, which gives a greater level of newness to its collections," says Anne Critchlow, a retail analyst at Société Générale.

8 About two-thirds of Inditex's products are generated under short lead times, vs. 20 percent for most retailers, she says. Small production runs mean Zara can test designs in various markets without building up unwanted stock that it might need to unload at a deep discount. That gives Inditex among the lowest yearend inventories in the industry, says Richard Hyman, an independent analyst in London. "This is a business that really breaks the rules," Hyman says. "They don't really have seasons in the way a normal fashion retailer would."

(Nov. 23, 2016 *Bloomberg Businessweek*)

Notes

1. **discernible hierarchy**「明白な階層。上の者が指揮命令をするような明白な階層的統括のこと」 **Arteixo**「アルテイショ。スペイン北部のガリシア州に位置し、北は大西洋に面する自治体。ガリシア州では重要な工業地帯でもあるが、Zara を展開するアパレルメーカーである Inditex の本社があることでも知られる」 **far-flung**「（地理的に）遠隔の」

2. **a breakaway success**「（他と異なる）飛び抜けた成功」 **file for bankruptcy**「破産申請を出す」 **a magic formula**「魔法の方式・手法、常套手段」

3. **Banco Popular Español**「1926 年創立の金融組織で、スペインで 6 番目の規模の組織であったが、2017 年にスペイン最大の商業銀行グループである Banco Santander に買収された」

4. **UBS**「スイスのチューリッヒおよびバーゼルに本社を持つ金融組織。投資業務、証券業務、資産運用を主たる業務とし、世界有数の地位を誇る」 **quick turnarounds**「商品の回転スピードの速さ、納期の速さ」

5. **much-vaunted**「評価の高い」

6. **augment**「増加させる」 **rapid-fire shoots**「立て続けに撮られる写真」 **sift through**「〜をふるいにかける」

7. **constantly tinker**「常時工夫する」 **tweak**「微調整する」 **generate so much buzz**「熱狂的な流行となる」 **churn out**「〜を大量に作り出す」 **lead time**「リードタイム。製品の企画・立案から製造までの時間」 **Société Générale**「フランスのメガバンクで、銀行、証券、投資信託業務を世界的に展開している」

8. **unload**「（在庫を）処分する」 **lowest yearend inventories**「最も少ない年度末余剰在庫」

Key Terms

Chief Executive Officer (CEO)
　最高経営責任者（主にアメリカで使われる役職名）。業務執行役員のトップであり、経営の方針や戦略の決定を行い、最終責任を負う。イギリスでは、managing directory あるいは chief executive（業務執行役員）が使われる。

fast fashion
　低価格で流行を採り入れた衣料品（ファッション）を、短いサイクルで大量生産・販売する製造小売業。Zara の他には UNIQLO、GU、H&M、GAP、Forever 21 などが挙げられる。

supply chain
　サプライチェーン、供給連鎖（原材料・部品の調達から、製造、在庫管理、販売、配送までの製品の一連の工程）。

Grasp the Main Points

本文の内容と合っているものには T、異なっているものには F を書き入れましょう。

1. The chief designer at Zara approves the new design of clothes and campaigns every year. ( )
2. Amancio Ortega, CEO of Inditex, is currently the world's richest man, outperforming Bill Gates. ( )
3. Zara has factories nearby, so the orders are delivered to stores quickly. ( )
4. Inditex spends a huge amount of money on advertising in magazines and on social media. ( )
5. Zara can test designs in a short period of time in different markets to avoid carrying an unwanted stock of clothes. ( )

Look for Specific Information

本文の内容に関して、次の選択肢問題に答えましょう。

1. Which of the following statement is true?
    a. Global clothing retailers are following the latest fashion trend in New York and copying Zara's culture.
    b. Inditex has developed a magic formula it follows in fashion business.
    c. Designers at Zara create new styles of clothes based on the daily data of sales of popular fashion items coming from around the world.
    d. For the global apparel business, the analysis of big data of trendy fashion is more important than designers' taste and judgment.

2. What is Zara's strategy in managing its growth?
    a. It is rapidly expanding its business around the world.
    b. It is focusing on big stores in main locations as well as its online business.
    c. It has doubled the number of stores in Europe since 2009.
    d. It is trying to catch up with the online sales of other major clothing retailers.

3. What does Zara do with clothes that are popular with customers?
    a. It continues to produce more of those popular clothes with the same design and color.
    b. It shortens the lead time of producing the popular items.
    c. It publishes popular clothes on Instagram and encourages customers to buy them.
    d. It creates other items in a similar style with different fabrics and prints.

Find Further Information

本文に基づいて、次のファッションブランドの経営状況について答えましょう。

1. American Apparel

   _____

2. GAP

   _____

3. Inditex (Zara's parent company)

   _____

Dictation & Conversation Practice　　　CD1-10

音声を聞いて空欄を埋め、会話をペアで練習しましょう。

In the coffee shop, Lisa and Scott are talking about fashion and shopping.

Lisa: Hey Scott, where do you usually go shopping for your clothes?

Scott: I usually shop at UNIQLO. The prices are reasonable and the materials they use are very good. 1._____. How about you?

Lisa: I like fast fashion too, but I usually shop at Zara.

Scott: How is Zara different from other fast fashion stores?

Lisa: Zara 2._____. They have so many designers working at the company and you can really see a difference in the styles of the clothes.

Scott: 3._____?

Lisa: They're about the same.

Scott: I really like 4._____. I especially like how the neck can be turned up or down. Is that from Zara?

Lisa: Yes, it is. See, the design is just a little different, but 5._____.

Scott: I see what you mean. You look good in that sweater.

What Do You Think...?　▶次のトピックについて、クラスメートと話し合いましょう。

1. What kind of similarities and differences do you find among Zara, UNIQLO, and H&M?
2. What impact do you think the fast fashion industry has on people's lives or the environment if people buy clothes and wear them only for a short period of time?

02

"Airbnb was not the first firm to pursue the concept of alternatives to hotels, but it was the first to become a global success."

Airbnb's Challenge and New Direction
民泊ビジネスにおける課題と挑戦

民泊ビジネスは最近日本でも知られるようになったが、このアイデアを世界規模で広めたのは Airbnb だ。個人宅での宿泊はホテル滞在と異なり、現地の住民の暮らしを垣間見ることができる。しかし、民泊の登録数が増えるにつれて様々な問題も浮上している。Airbnb が直面している課題、そして今後に向けての新たな取り組みとはどのようなものなのか。

Before You Read

トピックに関する次の質問に答えましょう。

1. Where do you usually stay when you travel in Japan or overseas? Do you make reservations by yourself or through a travel agency?
2. Have you ever stayed at one of the places Airbnb offers? If you have, how did you like your experience? If you haven't, would you like to stay at an Airbnb listing in the future?

Vocabulary

単語の日本語訳を選択肢より選び、その記号を記入しましょう。余分な選択肢が2つあります。

1. accommodation (   ) 6. comply   (   )
2. evolve   (   ) 7. breach   (   )
3. pitfall   (   ) 8. alternative (   )
4. launch   (   ) 9. forgo   (   )
5. impose   (   ) 10. aspiration (   )

a. 課す	d. 許す	g. 熱望、強い願望	j. 従う、遵守する
b. 侵害、違反	e. 代替	h. 開始する	k. 宿泊施設
c. なしで済ませる	f. 進化・発展する	i. 落とし穴	l. 停止する

Read the Article

1 Last year 80 million people booked stays on Airbnb, a platform for booking overnight stays in other people's homes, double the number in 2015. It now plans to expand into other bits of the market for accommodation, including luxury trips and business travel. New products, such as bespoke city tours, are in the works.

2 The firm's ultimate aim is to evolve from being a platform for overnight stays into a comprehensive travel company, capturing an ever-greater share of tourists' spending. In 2017 it may notch up as much as $2.8 billion in sales, up by around 65 percent from a year earlier; forecasts suggest it could reach $8.5 billion in revenues by 2020. An IPO may be in the offing, yet pitfalls also lie in wait. Chief among these is regulation, ensuring guests' safety and, increasingly, the need to fend off rivals such as Priceline, a fearsomely efficient online travel-booking company.

3 Airbnb's founders started as complete outsiders to the hospitality business and indeed, to commerce. Brian Chesky, its 35-year-old chief executive, had no previous business experience or technical expertise. Instead, he and one of his co-founders, Joe Gebbia, had studied design at Rhode Island School of Design before teaming up with a software engineer, Nathan Blecharczyk, to launch what was then called AirBed and Breakfast, with the aim of renting out air mattresses in apartments. They were so untutored in investing that when an early adviser suggested raising money from small investors known as "angels", Mr. Chesky thought people in Silicon Valley believed in celestial beings.

4 Airbnb's founders were early to recognise the importance of a strong, benign culture. Until 2013 the founders interviewed every job applicant, and today anyone who is hired still has to pass a "core values" interview, where they are judged not on their CV but on how they fit into the firm's sensibility. Asked whether Airbnb is a technology or a travel company, Vlad Loktev, its director of product, looks cautious. "We're more of a community company," he says.

5 Lobbying by the hotel industry has contributed to Airbnb's most obvious challenge, which is regulation. Opposition to the firm is fierce in many big cities, especially those with limited affordable housing, where residents blame Airbnb for taking apartments off the market. Several cities that could supply large profits, including Berlin, Barcelona and New York, have imposed rules that make offering short-term rentals difficult. New York, which is Airbnb's third-largest market, has banned short-term rentals in apartment buildings for less than 30 days, unless a host is present. Berlin has passed a de facto ban, by requiring a permit if someone wants to rent more than half of their apartment on a short-term basis and levying hefty fines for violations.

6 Airbnb has now opted for a new, more conciliatory approach, notes Leigh Gallagher, author of a book, *The Airbnb Story*. In Amsterdam and London it has agreed to police its listings to ensure they comply with local laws on the number of days a year each unit can be rented. Yet many investors worry that more restrictive laws will dampen its prospects.

7 A second, ever-present risk is safety. The platform functions because people trust that user photos and blind reviews will help root out bad actors. It faced a crisis in 2011 when Airbnb guests trashed a host's apartment and she blogged about the experience. Airbnb responded by offering insurance to all hosts of up to $1 million in damages. There remains the possibility of a dramatic breach in personal security, which could spook hosts and users.

8 The third threat is growing competition. Airbnb was not the first firm to pursue the concept of alternatives to hotels, but it was the first to become a global success. That has drawn the attention of others. In many markets, including China and Europe, Airbnb faces competition from local firms, as well as from established global players. In 2015 Expedia, an online-travel website, bought HomeAway, an Airbnb rival, for a hefty $3.9 billion.

9 But Airbnb's most fearsome competitor is Priceline, which owns Booking.com and is considered one of the best-managed Internet companies in the world. Priceline has been speedily adding alternative accommodation.

10 The travel industry is a large prize to share. Globally, people spend around $700 billion a year on travel accommodation, according to Euromonitor International, a research firm. With rising incomes and smaller families globally, travel is ever more popular. Many more people than first thought have been willing to forgo hotel luxuries such as gyms and concierges to get the proper feel of a place. That suggests that alternative accommodation will not be a fringe activity for the young, but a mainstream part of the travel business.

11 In any case, Airbnb's aspirations do not end there. It has created an innovation and design lab, called Samara, with the ambition of creating a new kind of travel offering. Last autumn Airbnb started selling "experiences", which are customised activities that travellers can book, including special meals, tours and exercise programmes, typically arranged by Airbnb hosts.

(May 27, 2017 *The Economist*)

Notes

1. **bespoke city tours**「オーダーメイドのシティツアー、顧客の要望に合わせた特別なツアー」
2. **notch up**「(成功・勝利などを)得る」 **in the offing**「やがて起こりそうな状態で」 **fend off rivals**「ライバルをかわす」 **Priceline**「アメリカのコネチカット州に拠点を置く最大級の売上高を誇るオンライン旅行会社」
3. **celestial beings**「天人、(同文中の angel のように) 人間ではなく天界に住んでいる者」
4. **benign culture**「人間味のある(企業)文化」
5. **a de facto ban**「事実上の禁止。"de facto" はラテン語で "from the fact" の意」 **levy hefty fines**「高額の罰金を徴収する」
6. **opt for**「〜を選択する」 **conciliatory approach**「懐柔的なアプローチ。困難な状況から巧みに切り抜ける対策」 **police**「監視する、取り締まる」
7. **root out**「〜を根絶する」 **spook**「脅す」
8. **HomeAway**「アメリカのテキサス州オースティンで始まったバケーション・レンタルサービス会社」
10. **a fringe activity**「付随的・付加的なアクティビティ。二次的な活動」

Key Terms

IPO (Initial Public Offering)

新規公開株、新規上場株式。株を投資家に売り出し、証券取引所で上場し、一般の投資家でも株の取引・売買をすることができるようにすること。

Silicon Valley

アメリカ、カリフォルニア州のサンフランシスコ・ベイエリアに位置しているサンタクララバレーとその周辺地域一帯の名称。半導体(Silicon)メーカーや最先端技術を有するIT企業の一大拠点となっている。

Expedia

アメリカのワシントン州に拠点を置く最大級のオンライン旅行会社。オンライン旅行予約サイトのほか、世界各地で事業を展開する企業も統括。日本語対応のコンテンツ運営はシンガポールで行っている。

Booking.com

オランダのアムステルダムにある、宿泊施設のオンライン予約サービスを提供するウェブサイトを運営する会社。サイトは宿泊予約の分野で世界最大の利用実績を持つ。親会社である Priceline は 2018 年に名称をブッキング・ホールディングス(Booking Holdings Inc.)に変更している。

02 Airbnb's Challenge and New Direction

Grasp the Main Points

本文の内容と合っているものには T、異なっているものには F を書き入れましょう。

1. Airbnb has offered places to stay in other people's homes to both luxury travelers and business people since 2015. ( )
2. Airbnb's founders studied hospitality business and software development at university. ( )
3. New York City prohibits less than one month stays at somebody's house under any conditions. ( )
4. Airbnb faces competition from not only local hotels but also from globally established chains. ( )
5. Airbnb has started to offer tailored programs that individual customers can enjoy while they travel. ( )

Look for Specific Information

本文の内容に関して、次の選択肢問題に答えましょう。

1. What qualities does Airbnb evaluate in hiring new employees?
    a. Their previous job experiences
    b. Their language skills
    c. Their software programming skills
    d. Their fitness in the company's culture

2. What measurements has Airbnb decided to take for damages caused by renters?
    a. It has decided to penalize the renters who damage the host's property.
    b. It has decided to ban customers from using its service in the future.
    c. It has decided to offer insurance to hosts to cover damages.
    d. It has decided to provide new furniture if the host asks for it.

3. How much do people around the world spend on travel accommodation a year?
    a. $2.8 billion
    b. $3.9 billion
    c. $8.5 billion
    d. $700 billion

11

Find Further Information

本文に基づいて、Airbnb の直面する 3 つの課題について答えましょう。

1. Regulation
   _____

2. Safety
   _____

3. Competition
   _____

Dictation & Conversation Practice CD1-22

音声を聞いて空欄を埋め、会話をペアで練習しましょう。

Eric is asking Sue about her trip to New York and her accommodation arrangements.

Eric: Hi Sue. I heard you were going to New York next week for a short vacation.

Sue: Yeah. My friends and I are going there for five days. It's our first time and 1._____.

Eric: Sounds fun. New York has a lot of great hotels. Where are you staying?

Sue: Well, we've decided to use Airbnb and stay in a one bedroom condo right downtown. Airbnb has so many choices available. Have you ever tried it?

Eric: Yes, I have. In fact, I often use them when I travel. I think they should 2._____.

Sue: Interesting. What kind of services?

Eric: In addition to lodging, they could provide itinerary guides for touring around the area, 3._____, and even personal tour guides.

Sue: That's a great idea. Airbnb could provide a platform for all kinds of travel and tourist services.

Eric: That would be nice. They could 4._____.

Sue: Maybe, we will see them 5._____ in the near future.

What Do You Think...? ▶次のトピックについて、クラスメートと話し合いましょう。

1. Why do you think some people choose Airbnb accommodations, instead of hotels? What are some problems you may have when staying at someone's private house or apartment?

2. What are some new services you think Airbnb could offer in the future?

"We want to get to this world in the future where you can mix digital or physical objects in the digital world."

Augmented Reality Ecosystem in Facebook
拡張現実の構築で世界を変える？

世界中でおよそ 20 億人のユーザーがいると言われている Facebook は、世界最大級のソーシャル・ネットワーキング・サービスである。この Facebook を利用して友人、同僚、家族、知人が繋がり、ネット上で様々な交流をすることが可能になった。しかし、Apple や Google のように製品やサービスを提供しているわけではない Facebook は、IT 業界の次なるフロンティアとして何を目指そうとしているのだろうか。

Before You Read

トピックに関する次の質問に答えましょう。

1. Do you use social media sites? If you do, what sites do you use (e.g. Facebook, Instagram, WhatsApp, Messenger, Twitter, etc.)?
2. If you use social media sites, on what occasions do you post your comments, pictures, or videos? How often do you check others' posts?

Vocabulary

単語の日本語訳を選択肢より選び、その記号を記入しましょう。余分な選択肢が２つあります。

1. manipulate   (   )   6. scrutiny   (   )
2. nascent   (   )   7. entice   (   )
3. envision   (   )   8. emulate   (   )
4. flop   (   )   9. abandon   (   )
5. grapple   (   )   10. acquisition (   )

a. 初期段階の	**d.** 誘う、気をひく	**g.** 達成	**j.** 模倣する
b. 精査、調査	**e.** 買収、取得	**h.** 騙す	**k.** 廃止する
c. 失敗する	**f.** 操る、操作する	**i.** 取り組む	**l.** 予見する

Read the Article

[1] Facebook's chief executive, Mark Zuckerberg, has long rued the day that Apple and Google beat him to building smartphones, which now underpin many people's digital lives. Ever since, he has searched for the next frontier of modern computing and how to be a part of it from the start.

[2] Now, Mr. Zuckerberg is betting he has found it: the real world. Mr. Zuckerberg introduced what he positioned as the first mainstream augmented reality platform, a way for people to view and digitally manipulate the physical world around them through the lens of their smartphone cameras.

[3] What that means today is fairly limited. Augmented reality is nascent — people can add simple flourishes on top of their photos or videos, like sticking a pixelated blue beard on a selfie or adding puppy stickers to a photo of the front yard of their house.

[4] But in Mr. Zuckerberg's telling, there are few boundaries for how this technology will evolve. He said he envisioned a world in which people could eventually point smartphone cameras at a bowl of cereal and have an app create tiny sharks swimming in the milk. Friends can leave virtual notes for one another on the walls outside their favorite restaurants, noting which menu item is the most delicious.

[5] Apps like Pokémon Go, the augmented reality game that was a global hit last year, are just the beginning for Mr. Zuckerberg. One day, he mused, household objects could perhaps be replaced entirely by software. Mr. Zuckerberg's goal is ambitious. Augmented reality efforts have flopped in the past, including Google's much-promoted attempt around spectacles with the technology, known as Google Glass. Facebook has previously gambled on other futuristic technologies — including virtual reality, with a $2 billion purchase of Oculus, the virtual reality goggles maker, in 2014 — but Mr. Zuckerberg has acknowledged that it has had difficulty finding traction.

[6] He is also grappling with many issues that have the potential to distract Facebook. The company is under scrutiny for its position as an arbiter of mass media and faces questions as to what role Facebook should play in policing content across its platform of nearly two billion regular users. Still, Mr. Zuckerberg said he intended to create the next major app ecosystem that would work with Facebook's in-app camera. If successful, Facebook could be in a position similar to that of Apple, which relies on the hundreds of millions of apps in its store to keep users buying the company's smartphones and tablets every year.

[7] Facebook, in turn, wants developers to build experiences that entice people to visit its website and apps on a daily — if

not hourly — basis. "Just like Apple built the iPod and iTunes ecosystem before the iPhone, you want to make sure there's a set of content there, even if there's not everything," Mr. Zuckerberg said.

8 Facebook has been building toward this goal for some time. Mr. Zuckerberg has spent the last 18 months reorganizing his company and its suite of consumer apps — Facebook, Instagram, WhatsApp and Messenger — around a new interface, focused almost entirely on the camera. Slowly, the company has played down the role of text inside its apps, instead encouraging people to take and send photos and videos to one another by using the in-app camera features.

9 In time, Facebook hopes that companies like Electronic Arts, Nike and Warner Brothers — which are part of the initial set of partners — will be the ones to bring immersive augmented reality experiences to Facebook's platform. One early partner app is Giphy Thoughts, made by Giphy, a start-up that acts as a search engine for animated GIFs, which play as something like short-form videos. With Giphy Thoughts, for instance, people can place cartoon thought bubbles above the heads of others they view through their Facebook camera lens.

10 Facebook's past attempts to be at the center of an apps ecosystem with developers have not been particularly successful. In 2012, the company released App Center, a hub within Facebook to discover third-party apps — like FarmVille, Goodreads and Spotify — and use them on the Facebook desktop site. But that initiative fizzled as consumers slowly shifted away from desktops to smartphones.

11 One year later, Facebook tried to emulate Apple's and Google's platform strategies more directly with its own branded smartphone, called Facebook Home. The phone, a product of a partnership with AT&T and HTC, sold poorly and was eventually abandoned.

12 Then came Facebook's most aggressive move, the acquisition of Oculus in 2014. Facebook is investing hundreds of millions of dollars more in V.R. content and apps in the hopes that it will mature into a full-fledged ecosystem similar to Apple's App Store, but sales of the Oculus Rift goggles have been slow.

13 For the near term, however, Mr. Zuckerberg sees the smartphone camera as the first step forward. "We want to get to this world in the future where you eventually have glasses or contact lenses where you can mix digital or physical objects in the digital world," he said.

(Apr. 18, 2017 *The New York Times*)

Notes

1. rue「後悔する、残念に思う」 underpin「（根底から）支える」
3. flourishes「飾り書き、飾り線文様」 pixelated「ピクセル化された。ピクセル化とは、画像の質に大きな変化をもたらせ、その印象を一変させてしまうフィルタ機能」
5. muse「熟考する」 traction「魅力」
6. distract「混乱させる」 arbiter「権威者」
8. suite of「一連の」
9. Electronic Arts「1982年に設立された、アメリカのカリフォルニア州にあるビデオ・コンピューターゲームの販売会社」 animated GIFs「ジフ画像。Graphics Interchange Format の略で、画像ファイル形式の一つ。複数の画像をまとめることで、ファイル形式は画像でありつつも、パラパラ漫画のような短いアニメーションを作ることができる」
10. FarmVille「2009年に発売され、『のんびり農場生活』の名前で親しまれているシミュレーションビデオゲーム」 Goodreads「Amazonが2006年に開設した、書籍情報や批評、推薦図書を閲覧することができるウェブサイト」 Spotify「音楽のストリーミング配信サービスを提供・運営する企業。2006年創立で、本社はスウェーデンのストックホルム。業界世界大手で、2016年より日本でもサービスが開始された」 fizzle「立ち消えに終わる」
11. AT&T「アメリカ最大手の電話会社。ネットワーク、セキュリティ、および映像配信サービスなども提供し、近年ではIoT (Internet of Things) をグローバルに展開している」 HTC「エイチ・ティー・シー・コーポレーション。台湾で創立された携帯端末機器の製造業者。これまで日本では主にNTT、ソフトバンク、auなどに製品を提供」
12. full-fledged「本格的な、十分な、成熟した」

Key Terms

augmented reality
　拡張現実。人が知覚する現実環境をコンピューターにより拡張する技術、またはコンピューターにより拡張された現実環境そのもの。

virtual reality
　仮想現実。コンピューターが作った人工の仮想空間に入って、あたかも現実かのように体験する技術・システム。

ecosystem
　エコシステムはもともと「生態系」を意味する言葉であるが、ビジネス分野の特定の業界の複数企業が協調、連携することによって業界全体としての収益構造を維持しようとするシステムをここでは意味する。

03 Augmented Reality Ecosystem in Facebook

▌Grasp the Main Points
本文の内容と合っているものには T、異なっているものには F を書き入れましょう。

1. Augmented reality is still in the primitive stage where people enjoy adding some stickers to their photos. ( )
2. The augmented reality platform that Facebook created has enabled people to see digital creatures in the food you eat. ( )
3. Facebook would like to create its own app ecosystem like Apple where users continue to buy apps and products. ( )
4. Facebook is planning to increase the role of text inside its apps so that people can add more messages to their photos and videos. ( )
5. Facebook's smartphone, "Facebook Home" eventually became a big hit. ( )

▌Look for Specific Information
本文の内容に関して、次の選択肢問題に答えましょう。

1. What kind of augmented reality devices or apps have not yet caught on?
    a. Pokémon Go
    b. WhatsApp
    c. Google Glass
    d. Instagram

2. What can people do with Giphy Thoughts?
    a. Create animated characters in the movies.
    b. Add thought bubbles above people in the videos.
    c. Make cartoons in the digital books.
    d. Create sound effects in the animations.

3. Why has App Center, created on the Facebook desktop site, lost its popularity?
    a. Because people have started to use more smartphones than desktops.
    b. Because people have become more interested in third-party apps on the desktops.
    c. Because it was hard to use Oculus Rift goggles.
    d. Because the apps in the App Center were too expensive.

Find Further Information

本文に基づいて、Facebook が提供する次の製品・サービスについて答えましょう。

1. Facebook Home
   _____

2. Oculus Rift
   _____

Dictation & Conversation Practice   CD1-36

音声を聞いて空欄を埋め、会話をペアで練習しましょう。

Mayu, a Japanese university student, is showing Kent, an exchange student from Canada, around Kyoto.

Mayu: Kent, this shrine has a long history in Kyoto and there are [1]._____ _____ connected with it.

Kent: It looks beautiful. What is this main gate called?

Mayu: "Torii." It represents [2]._____ _____.

Kent: Look here, there's an English sign. Let's read what it says.

Mayu: Okay. It says that if you use this app and [3]._____ _____ around the shrine, then stories and pictures will appear.

Kent: Fabulous. The city is using augmented reality software to add more information to many tourist sites. Let's try it.

Mayu: Here's a sign marker. Wow, look at that. A story about this shrine appears in [4]._____.

Kent: I'm impressed. It's such a traditional place with such modern technology.

Mayu: This is really cool. [5]._____ _____ and adds a new level of information. It makes me want to learn more.

What Do You Think...? ▶次のトピックについて、クラスメートと話し合いましょう。

1. Have you ever used AR (augmented reality)? What was your experience like? If you haven't, would you like to try AR?

2. AR can be used at tourist spots to give more information. What are some other ways that AR could be used?

"In the history of sneaker making, this is probably the biggest revolution."

Adidas Brings the Fast Shoe Revolution One Step Closer
「超高速」靴製造の技術革新

ドイツのバイエルン州に本社を置くスポーツ用品メーカーAdidas。創業者のアドルフの愛称、「アディ」と名字の「ダスラー」を繋げて、「アディダス」と名付けられた。サッカー日本代表のユニフォームも手がけている世界的なブランドである。多くの衣料品や靴の製造が賃金の安いアジアで行われている中、Adidasは革新的な技術の導入で、新たな靴作りの実現を可能にした。

Before You Read

トピックに関する次の質問に答えましょう。

1. When and where do you usually buy your regular shoes or sports shoes?
2. Is there a particular brand of shoes you like? Explain why or why not.

Vocabulary

単語の日本語訳を選択肢より選び、その記号を記入しましょう。余分な選択肢が2つあります。

1. facility　　　(　)
2. supplier　　　(　)
3. defect　　　(　)
4. prototype　　　(　)
5. hype　　　(　)
6. attribute　　　(　)
7. variant　　　(　)
8. adhesion　　　(　)
9. exclusive　　　(　)
10. negligible　　　(　)

a. 高揚感、売り込み	d. 専属の	g. 接着	j. 施設、設備
b. 流れる、逃げる	e. 納入業者	h. 顧客	k. 特性、特質
c. 異なる版・型	f. 重要な	i. 取るに足らない	l. 原型、モデル

Read the Article

1 In a production hall as clean as a hospital, pea-size beads of white plastic pour into what looks like a minivan-size Adidas shoe box, complete with three white stripes down the side. That's fitting, because in just a few seconds the machine heats and molds the stuff into soles of Adidas running shoes, with only one worker needed to wedge in pieces of plastic called stability bars. This is Adidas AG's "Speedfactory," where the shoemaker aims to prove it can profitably produce footwear in high-cost, developed economies. By next fall the facility, as large as half a soccer field, will employ about 160 people to make 1,500 pairs of shoes a day, or 500,000 annually.

2 The plant, halfway between Munich and Frankfurt, and a twin opening this fall near Atlanta, will be key to Adidas's effort to catch industry leader Nike Inc. It replaces manual stitching and gluing with molding and bonding done by machines, churning out running shoes in a day, vs. two or three months in China and Vietnam, where components are shuttled among suppliers that produce individual parts. "In the history of sneaker making, this is probably the biggest revolution since manufacturing moved to Asia," James Carnes, a 23-year Adidas veteran responsible for company strategy, says as he tours the plant. "Or maybe since sport shoes were made."

3 The factories take a page from fast-fashion pioneers Zara and H&M, part of an effort by Adidas to more quickly get shoes, soccer jerseys, and other goods from designers' sketchbooks to store shelves. Adidas says coupling speed with customization will allow it to sell more gear at full price and keep customers from defecting to rivals. It used a prototype of the Speedfactory to manufacture a running shoe called "Futurecraft Made for Germany," a big hit a year ago, with buyers camping outside stores to get one of just 500 pairs at €249 ($293) apiece.

4 Adidas is betting it can repeat the hype with similar city-themed shoes to be made at the two Speedfactories: London and Paris this fall, and New York, Los Angeles, Tokyo, and Shanghai next year. Each version, planned in batches of several thousand pairs, features attributes Adidas says are tailored to the needs of a city's runners. "AM4LDN adidas Made For London" will have reflectors and beefed-up waterproofing for jogging in the dark and rain, the Los Angeles model is designed for hotter weather, and the Shanghai variant will be adapted for indoor tracks popular there. In each instance, the shoes are designed to be made by machines, not by hand, and Adidas gains the added benefit of keeping the latest trends and ideas in-house rather than sharing them with suppliers. "Our industry is extremely competitive, so new things have an enormous value," says Gerd Manz, who oversees technology innovation at Adidas.

"Our goal is to use this as a launching ground for innovation."

5 Adidas's rivals are pursuing similar strategies, with Nike investing in a company making electrical adhesion machines that can assemble the upper part of a shoe 20 times faster than a human worker can. New Balance Athletics Inc. and Under Armour Inc. have started 3D-printing parts of the soles of some shoes. And Feetz Inc., based in San Diego, says it can 3D-print custom shoes for buyers who send in photos of their feet.

6 Athletics brands today are mostly design and marketing machines that leave the stitching and gluing to subcontractors. Adidas hasn't owned any big factories since the 1990s, but its suppliers employ more than 1 million people at 1,000-plus facilities in 63 countries. While the company is developing the technology used in the Speedfactories, the plants will be owned and operated by Germany's Oechsler AG, an exclusive Adidas supplier.

7 The Speedfactories won't necessarily mean fewer jobs at Adidas's suppliers. With the company's projected 10 percent to 12 percent annual growth rate requiring an additional 40 million pairs of shoes annually through 2020, the contribution of the automated plants will be negligible. But, if they prove successful, Adidas may add more or expand capacity to 2.5 million pairs a year at each of the current factories. It's also considering offering the technology and processes to subcontractors so they can boost automation as wages rise. "The framework in Germany today, the social, environmental, legal requirements, are just what we will also see in our sourcing countries in a few years," Manz says. "We'll be prepared."

(Oct. 5, 2017 Bloomberg Businessweek)

Notes

1. **wedge**「押し込む」 **Adidas AG**「アディダスの正式英語名称。AG はドイツ語で株式会社を意味する。1949年創立」
2. **Nike Inc.**「アメリカのオレゴン州に本社を置く世界的スポーツ用品メーカー。1964年創立」
3. **take a page from**「～を見習う、模倣する」 **Zara**「スペインのガリシア州に本部を置く、Inditex が展開する世界有数のファッションブランド。1975年に1号店を開店」 **H&M**「スウェーデンのストックホルムに本社を置くH & M Hennes & Mauritz AB が展開するファストファッションブランド。1947年創立」
4. **batches of**「何組もの」 **reflectors**「反射面」 **beefed-up**「強化された、増強された」
5. **New Balance Athletics Inc.**「アメリカのマサチューセッツ州ボストンに本社を置くスポーツシューズメーカー。1906年創立」 **Under Armour Inc.**「アメリカのメリーランド州ボルチモアに本社を置くスポーツ用品メーカー。1996年創立」 **Feetz Inc.**「アメリカのカリフォルニア州サンディエゴに本社を置くカスタム・メイドのシューズメーカー。インソールに3Dプリントを活用する企業が出現する中、3Dプリントによる靴の完全なカスタマイズ商品を特徴とする」
6. **subcontractors**「下請け業者」 **Oechsler AG**「エクスラー・モーション。ドイツのアンスバッハに本社を置き、射出成形の精密プラスチック部品や電気機械部品の設計・製造をする企業」

Key Terms

developed economies
　先進国、先進経済・先進工業国。developed nations や developed countries のような表記も多い。
　これらに対して、発展途上国は developing nations や developing countries という。

athletics brands
　スポーツウェアやシューズを扱うブランド。

sourcing countries
　部品調達国。部品および材料の仕入れ先の国。

04 Adidas Brings the Fast Shoe Revolution One Step Closer

Grasp the Main Points

本文の内容と合っているものには T、異なっているものには F を書き入れましょう。

1. Adidas is going to open two Speedfactories in Germany to compete with Nike. （　）
2. Adidas learned the idea of quickly producing shoes and jerseys from fast-fashion companies. （　）
3. Adidas is planning to manufacture shoes for city runners in Europe first, and later in the US and Asia. （　）
4. Sports brands nowadays mostly design and market products while their subcontractors make shoes. （　）
5. The construction of more Speedfactories means that there will be fewer jobs at Adidas's suppliers. （　）

Look for Specific Information

本文の内容に関して、次の選択肢問題に答えましょう。

1. How many pairs of shoes is the new Adidas factory expected to produce per day?
   a. 500 pairs of shoes
   b. 1,500 pairs of shoes
   c. 5,000 pairs of shoes
   d. 50,000 pairs of shoes

2. What is the name of shoes made in a Speedfactory that became very popular a year ago?
   a. AM4LDN adidas Made for London
   b. The Biggest Revolution in London
   c. The Framework in Germany
   d. Futurecraft Made for Germany

3. Besides quick manufacturing of products, what is the benefit of producing shoes by machines?
   a. They can keep the trends and design ideas within the company.
   b. They can share their designs with suppliers around the world.
   c. They don't need to offer the technology assistant to subcontractors.
   d. They can ship parts to China and Vietnam quickly.

Find Further Information

本文に基づいて、Adidas の Speedfactory について次の質問に答えましょう。

1. How large is the Speedfactory?
   _____

2. How many people will the Speedfactory employ?
   _____

3. What would Speedfactory make possible?
   _____

Dictation & Conversation Practice　　　　　　　　　　　　　🅞 CD1-44

音声を聞いて空欄を埋め、会話をペアで練習しましょう。

Chris and Mary are talking about "made-to-measure" shoes.

Chris: Have you heard of "made-to-measure" shoes?
Mary: No, I haven't. ¹_____?
Chris: You could say that. You put your feet in a special machine for a complete measurement of your feet. Then, ²_____
_____.
Mary: Cool. It's hard for me to find shoes that fit, so that would be helpful.
Chris: 3D technology is really developing. You can get measured and then a computer ³_____.
Mary: Is there any choice of color and design to the shoes you can buy with "made-to-measure"?
Chris: Yes, you can choose the color, design, and other details as well.
Mary: That's fantastic. I think I'll try that out. ⁴_____
_____.
Chris: You can have your own original style of shoes that nobody else has.
Mary: That would ⁵_____.

What Do You Think...?　▶次のトピックについて、クラスメートと話し合いましょう。

1. Would you like to try made-to-measure shoes? What do you think some of the merits and demerits of made-to-measure clothing and shoes might be?
2. Find out some labor issues at factories of global apparel companies in South East Asia. What do you think they should do to improve their factory workers' conditions?

"The company has resisted the very modern allure of automation."

EPA ＝時事

At Toyota, the Automation Is Human-Powered
自動車生産の自動化と職人技

日本が誇る世界的な自動車メーカーの Toyota。本社のある愛知県豊田市は、市名が企業名から付けられた希なケースである。Toyota 自動車の優れた生産方式は海外からも注目され、広く紹介されている。リーマン・ショックやリコール問題で一時期赤字に転落したが、V字回復し、「もっといいクルマづくり」の姿勢を鮮明にした。新しく導入した設計開発方針で、Toyota が目指すものは何か。

Before You Read

トピックに関する次の質問に答えましょう。

1. Do you have a driver's license? If you do, how often do you drive? If you don't, would you like to get a driver's license in the future?
2. What type of cars do you or your family drive? Do you like your/your family's car? Explain why you like or don't like your/your family's car.

Vocabulary

単語の日本語訳を選択肢より選び、その記号を記入しましょう。余分な選択肢が2つあります。

1. allure ( )
2. contrarian ( )
3. indispensable ( )
4. quaint ( )
5. ingenuity ( )
6. devoid ( )
7. ubiquitous ( )
8. forge ( )
9. eschew ( )
10. elusive ( )

a. 古風な、趣のある	d. 築く、作り出す	g. 避ける	j. 反対意見の人
b. 魅力、誘惑	e. 含む	h. 〜が欠けている	k. 分かりにくい
c. 至る所にある	f. 不要な	i. 必要不可欠な	l. 独創性、創意

25

Read the Article

1 Even as the automaker unveils an updated version of its vaunted production system, called the Toyota New Global Architecture (TNGA), the company has resisted the very modern allure of automation — a particularly contrarian stance to take in the car industry, which is estimated to be responsible for over half of commercial robot purchases in North America.

2 "Our automation ratio today is no higher than it was 15 years ago," Wil James, president of Toyota Motor Manufacturing in Kentucky, told me as we sat in his office above the 8.1-million-square-foot (170 football fields) factory. And that ratio was low to begin with: For at least the last 10 years, robots have been responsible for less than 8 percent of the work on Toyota's global assembly lines. "Machines are good for repetitive things," James continued, "but they can't improve their own efficiency or the quality of their work. Only people can." He added that Toyota has conducted internal studies comparing the time it took people and machines to assemble a car; over and over, human labor won.

3 Such thinking seems unorthodox but it's not surprising given Toyota's well-known manufacturing system, which was first popularized in *The Machine That Changed the World*, an unlikely best-seller in the early 1990s written by three MIT academics. Despite its dry subject, this book had a radical impact inside and outside of the business community — for the first time, unveiling the mysteries of Japanese industrial expertise and popularizing terms like lean production, continuous improvement, *andon* assembly lines, seven wastes or *mudas* and product flow.

4 Fundamentally, Toyota's production principles were keyed to the notion that people are indispensable, the eyes, ears, and hands on the assembly line — identifying problems, recommending creative fixes, and offering new solutions for enhancing the product or process. Today, that idea seems quaint. In the industrial world now manufacturing prowess is measured more by robotic agility than human ingenuity.

5 As an aspiration, lean is taking a back seat to lights-out — a manufacturing concept Elon Musk is championing for his Model 3 Tesla plant in which illumination will ultimately not be needed because the factory will be devoid of people. Even before we get there, auto companies like Kia — headquartered in Korea where the use of robots in manufacturing outpaces all other countries — are already claiming productivity improvements of nearly 200 percent from automation. Some plants have more than 1,000 robots — and less than a thousand people — on an assembly line. Indeed, a nearly fetishistic appreciation of automation is ubiquitous these days.

6 Dozens of articles, white papers, and books, written by respected thought leaders, executives, and consultants, depict an industrial future inevitably overrun by robots able to do the most sophisticated tasks at inhuman levels of efficiency. These are siren calls to most manufacturers whose growth plans are conditioned on cutting labor costs, which often make up as much as 25 percent of the value of their products.

7 An oft-quoted Oxford University analysis predicts that over the next two decades, some 47 percent of American jobs will be lost to automation. In China and India, that figure is even higher: 77 percent and 69 percent respectively.

8 But Toyota has forged a different path. The automaker, now jockeying with Volkswagen and Renault-Nissan for the top spot in worldwide sales, consistently generates industry best profit margins, often 8 percent or more. To maintain this performance, Toyota has eschewed seeking growth primarily through cost-cutting (through automation), but rather has focused on automobile improvements offered at aggressively competitive prices.

9 Codified as the Toyota New Global Architecture, this strategy doesn't primarily target labor to reduce production expenses but instead is weighted toward smarter use of materials; reengineering automobiles so their component parts are lighter and more compact and their weight distribution is maxed out for performance and fuel efficiency; more economical global sharing of engine and vehicle models (trimming back more than 100 different platforms to fewer than ten); and a renewed emphasis on elusive lean concepts, such as processes that allow assembly lines to produce a different car one after another with no downtime. In TNGA's framework, robots are not the strategic centerpiece, but merely enablers and handmaidens, helping assemblers do their jobs better, stimulating employee innovation and when possible facilitating cost gains.

10 As if to punctuate how old-school this way of thinking is today, Toyota made an unusual executive appointment in 2015. Unexpectedly, the automaker named Mitsuru Kawai, a 52-year veteran of the firm (he was hired at 15), to head up global manufacturing, the highest position ever held by a former blue-collar worker. Kawai is one of the last remaining links at Toyota to Taiichi Ohno, the godfather of lean manufacturing and the Toyota production system.

11 Kawai's job now is to imbue TNGA with Ohno's memory by bringing human craftsmanship back to the fore. Kawai described the manufacturing philosophy he uses to achieve this as uncomplicated: "Humans should produce goods manually and make the process as simple as possible. Then when the process is thoroughly simplified, machines can take over. But rather than gigantic multi-function robots, we should use equipment that is adept at single simple purposes."

(Sept. 5, 2017 Fast Company)

Notes

[3] *andon* assembly lines「Toyota の創意による品質管理法。*"andon"* は、『行灯（昔、周囲を照らすために使われた灯火道具）』からきている。この組み立てラインでは、問題があると警告信号によってその個所を知らされ、生産が停止された上で、問題処理が行われる。警告信号は主に生産者が手動で作動する。生産者にライン停止の権限を与えることにより、生産者の能力の尊重また勤労意欲の向上にも貢献すると言われる」

[4] agility「鋭敏、機敏、敏捷性」

[5] take a back seat to「〜の二番手に甘んじる、〜よりも重要でなくなる（後部席に座る）」 lights-out「完全自動の。照明器具が不要な状態でも操業可能である、という意味」 Elon Musk「イーロン・マスク。電気自動車会社テスラ、スペース・エクスプロレーション・テクノロジーズ（スペース X）社の共同設立者および CEO」 fetishistic「盲目的な」

[6] siren calls「興味をそそられる、魅惑的な誘惑」

[8] jockey with「〜と互いに有利な立場を得ようとする」 profit margins「利益率（利益額と売上高の比率）」

[9] codify「整備する、成文化する」 max out「〜を最大限に達する」

[10] punctuate「強調する、明確にする」

[11] imbue「吹き込む」

Key Terms

Toyota New Global Architecture (TNGA)

トヨタ・ニュー・グローバル・アーキテクチャー。Toyota 自動車による、商品力向上と原価低減を達成するための生産構想。プラットフォーム（複数の車種により共有される構成部品の組み合わせ）だけでなく、消費者の声を反映した企画、開発、調達も含めたすべての工程に関係する方針。

The Machine That Changed the World

邦訳『リーン生産方式が、世界の自動車産業をこう変える。』マサチューセッツ工科大学（MIT）が、1991年に車の未来について研究し、まとめた本。下記の lean production という語を生み出したのは本書。多くの言語に翻訳されている。

lean production

リーン生産方式。マサチューセッツ工科大学が、Toyota の無駄のない生産方式に着目して名付けたとされる。"lean" には「ぜい肉がなく引き締まっている」という意味がある。

05 At Toyota, the Automation Is Human-Powered

Grasp the Main Points

本文の内容と合っているものには T、異なっているものには F を書き入れましょう。

1. Wil James, President of Toyota in Kentucky, claims that machines are good at improving their efficiency of repetitive work. ( )
2. Some studies at Toyota showed that it took machines more time than people to assemble a car. ( )
3. Tesla and Kia rely heavily on their automation in producing automobiles. ( )
4. According to Oxford University analysis, more than half of American jobs will be lost to machines in twenty years. ( )
5. The new head of Toyota's global manufacturing thinks machines outweigh human craftsmanship in the company's production system. ( )

Look for Specific Information

本文の内容に関して、次の選択肢問題に答えましょう。

1. What is one of Toyota's major principles?
   a. Lights-out manufacturing is the key to efficiency.
   b. People are indispensable in improving the manufacturing process.
   c. Robotic agility is more important than human ingenuity.
   d. Factories will no longer need people.

2. Why will illumination not be necessary at the Tesla Model 3 plant?
   a. Because the factory will be mainly operated by machines.
   b. Because problems will be fixed outside the factory.
   c. Because people will work in the factory during the daytime.
   d. Because the plant will use solar energy.

3. What is one of the frameworks of TNGA (Toyota New Global Architecture)?
   a. It cuts the labor costs to reduce production expenses.
   b. It employs robots as the strategic centerpiece.
   c. It builds different assembly lines for different types of cars.
   d. It makes better use of component parts to produce fuel efficient vehicles.

Find Further Information

本文に基づいて、1990 年代の Toyota の評判と TNGA の指針について答えましょう。

1. Toyota in the 1990s
   _____

2. The main framework of TNGA (Toyota New Global Architecture)
   _____

Dictation & Conversation Practice   CD1-56

音声を聞いて空欄を埋め、会話をペアで練習しましょう。

Mike and Yuko are talking about shopping for a new car.

Mike: Let's go car shopping. ^{1.}_____
_____.

Yuko: Okay, sounds good to me. But there are so many choices.

Mike: Yes, there sure are. But, we have already decided to buy a small Japanese car, right? ^{2.}_____.

Yuko: I agree. Small and eco-friendly. The Japanese cars really are my favorite. ^{3.}_____.

Mike: I think they pay a lot of attention to the details in the design and manufacturing of the cars.

Yuko: I guess there is a nice combination of ^{4.}_____
_____ in the design process.

Mike: Now, we need to decide on which car and whether or not we should buy a regular, hybrid, or electric car.

Yuko: Okay. ^{5.}_____, then.

Mike: I hope we can make our decision soon. It's going to be fun to have a new car.

What Do You Think...? ▶次のトピックについて、クラスメートと話し合いましょう。

1. What would be your criteria for choosing a car? (e.g. price, function, size, color, style, safety, reliability, environmental concerns, gas mileage, domestic or foreign brands, etc.)?
2. What are the merits and demerits of using automation in the manufacturing of vehicles?

06

"When I walked in this store for the first time, I knew I was home."

AFP ＝時事

How Starbucks Became a Successful Worldwide Brand
グローバルブランドの原点と成功への道のり

アメリカのシアトルで第 1 号店を開いた Starbucks は、現在では世界の約 90 の国と地域で 2 万を超える店舗を構える。日本でも「スタバ」として親しまれ、多くの人に利用されている。世界規模のコーヒーショップチェーンとなった Starbucks の成功への道のりはどのようなものであったのだろうか。スターバックスコーポレーション会長・ハワード・シュルツが大切にしている原点とは何か。

Before You Read

トピックに関する次の質問に答えましょう。

1. Do you have a particular coffee/tea shop you like to visit in your town? If you do, how often do you go there? What do you usually order?
2. Do you like Starbucks? What's your favorite drink at Starbucks? Explain why you like it.

Vocabulary

単語の日本語訳を選択肢より選び、その記号を記入しましょう。余分な選択肢が 2 つあります。

1. compensation （ ）
2. institute （ ）
3. compelling （ ）
4. merge （ ）
5. acumen （ ）
6. embrace （ ）
7. diversity （ ）
8. accountability （ ）
9. compromise （ ）
10. execution （ ）

a. 鋭才、洞察力	**d.** 妥協	**g.** 補償	**j.** 人をひきつける
b. 受容する	**e.** 制定する	**h.** 実行	**k.** 多様性
c. 軽視する	**f.** 責務、責任	**i.** 課題	**l.** 合併する

Read the Article

1 Starbucks CEO Howard Schultz was seven years old and living in the Brooklyn projects with his two siblings when his father, a truck driver, broke his ankle. Without health insurance or worker's compensation, his family was left without an income or the ability to pay for medical bills. The family somehow got by but that experience was a defining moment for Schultz. Later, as the CEO of Starbucks, he instituted an unheard of health insurance program that offers health insurance to both full and part-time employees.

2 A talented athlete, Schultz got into Northern Michigan University on a football scholarship but ultimately decided not to play and got through school with loans and odd jobs. After college, he went into sales, and it was at his second company, Hammarplast, which sold European coffee makers, that led Schultz to Starbucks.

3 A compelling communicator, he'd risen within the company quickly. Starbucks, a tiny coffee bean selling operation, back then owned by Jerry Baldwin, Zev Siegl and Gordon Bowker — blipped onto his radar when Schultz, the director of sales, noticed an uptick of coffee maker sales to the company out in Seattle. Piqued, he flew out to the city to suss out the situation. "When I walked in this store for the first time — I know this sounds really hokey — I knew I was home," Schultz later remembered.

4 A year later, he joined the company as Starbucks' director of sales, and during a trip to Italy, he had an epiphany. Up until then, Starbucks had just sold coffee beans. However, struck by Italy's coffee bar culture, he became convinced that Starbucks should serve coffee drinks and foster community. In 1984, the original owners of Starbucks gave him the greenlight to open up one coffee bar in Seattle, which became a huge success. However, it soon became evident that Schultz had a very different idea of where to take the company, so he left to open a coffee bar chain of his own: Il Giornale.

5 Il Giornale also was successful, and Schultz was able to buy Starbucks and merge it with Il Giornale in 1987. Today, no coffee chain sells more coffee drinks to more people in more places.

6 The 62-year-old CEO — who was first to graduate from college in his family — is currently worth approximately $3 billion and heads the Schultz Family Foundation, which focuses on economic mobility for veterans and youth.

7 Schultz is a true radical and visionary for leadership and business acumen. Here are five lessons we can take away from this leader.

8 **1. Not every decision is an economic one.**

Schultz is a CEO who cares *deeply* about social change. In January 2012, he made his support for gay marriage clear when he publicly joined other big brands, such as Nike and Microsoft, in backing a Washington state bill to legalize same sex marriage. "The lens in which we are making that decision is through the lens of our people. We employ over 200,000 people in this company, and we want to embrace diversity. Of all kinds." It is clear that Schultz believes that Starbuck's accountability goes beyond merely financial.

2. Hire people you know who will challenge you.

Schultz has a tendency to micromanage. His strength is that he is aware of his control-freak tendencies, so he has countered this by shoring up his management team with leaders who can push back. In 2008, Schultz demanded that stores stop selling melted cheese breakfast sandwiches, saying that the strong cheddar scent was overpowering the scent of coffee. However, management pushed back — breakfast cheese sandwiches were popular — and a compromise was reached. The cheese sandwiches were reinstated, and the newer version heated at a lower temperature with smaller slices of medium cheddar instead of big slices of sharp cheddar — much to everyone's satisfaction.

3. Change the world — one crusade at a time.

Schultz is well known for his desire to do good, even if some results are bungled. While his execution of good intention may not always be fruitful, his concern about the country and politics have given rise to some successful and forward-thinking initiatives, some within his own company. Starbucks rolled out a program to pay for college tuition for its U.S. employees and funds 70 percent of health care costs for both full and part-time employees.

4. Stay connected to your roots.

Schultz stays connected to his past, not forgetting his humble beginnings in the Brooklyn projects. "I didn't go to an Ivy League school. I didn't go to business school," he says, when relating to the sorts of youth he employs. "I was one of those kids." He carries with him the key to the original flagship Starbucks store that opened in 1971 in Seattle's Pike's Place, where he first saw the brand's possibilities.

5. Earn the right to preach.

What he means is that you have to demonstrate that you can deliver the results as a trusted business leader first, with financial growth and profits, before pushing your social goals.

(June 30, 2016 *Entrepreneur*)

Notes

1. **the Brooklyn projects**「ブルックリン（ニューヨークにある5つの区のうちの一つ）の公共住宅」　**a defining moment**「決定的瞬間」
2. **odd jobs**「臨時の仕事、片手間仕事、雑用」　**Hammarplast**「スウェーデンの会社で、コーヒーメーカーの製造を主としていたが、財政難により1985年に閉業」
3. **blip onto his radar**「レーダーに現れる。ここでは Starbucks がシュルツの目に留まった、注意をひいたことを意味する」　**uptick**「上昇」　**pique**「興味をそそる、掻き立てる」　**suss out**「〜を偵察する」　**hokey**「センチメンタルな、感傷的な」
4. **epiphany**「直観」　**give 〜 the greenlight**「〜に正式に許可を与える」
8. **state bill**「州法案」
9. **shore up**「〜を支える、強化する」
10. **crusade**「改革」　**be bungled**「だめになる、やり損う」
11. **relate to**「〜に関わる、〜について話す」　**Pike's Place (Pike Place Market)**「パイク・プレイス・マーケット。スターバックスの第1号店はここに出店した」

Key Terms

Il Giornale
　シュルツが Starbucks を離れて設立したコーヒーチェーン。後にシュルツによって Starbucks と合併され、今の Starbucks となった。

Schultz Family Foundation
　1996年に教育、健康、医療などを含めた社会貢献を目的に設立された組織。特に若者の就業支援や、退役軍人の民間復帰支援を行う。

micromanage
　仕事を細かく管理し、部下が自分で決定を下す裁量をほとんど与えないトップダウン的なマネジメント方法。

06 How Starbucks Became a Successful Worldwide Brand

Grasp the Main Points

本文の内容と合っているものには T、異なっているものには F を書き入れましょう。

1. Starbucks provides health insurance programs that cover some costs for workers, regardless of their full-time or part-time status. ( )
2. After university, Schultz got his first job at a company that sold European coffee makers. ( )
3. Starbucks used to sell mainly coffee beans when Schultz first visited the store in Seattle. ( )
4. After Schultz became the director of sales at Starbucks, he found his ideas and the owners' ideas different and he left the company. ( )
5. The coffee shop Schultz started was not successful and that is why he decided to buy Starbucks in 1987. ( )

Look for Specific Information

本文の内容に関して、次の選択肢問題に答えましょう。

1. How did Schultz pay for his university education?
   a. He received a football scholarship to study at university.
   b. His parents helped him pay for his university education.
   c. He took out loans and worked part-time to pay for his university education.
   d. He received a scholarship from a private organization to study at university.

2. Why does Schultz care deeply about social change, including the legalization of gay marriage?
   a. Because he wants to join other big brands.
   b. Because he is well known for his desire to do good.
   c. Because he is financially responsible for his employees.
   d. Because he thinks diversity is important.

3. What does Schultz carry in order for him to stay connected to his past?
   a. His degree from an Ivy League school
   b. The key to the original Starbucks' store
   c. The program of the Brooklyn projects he was involved in
   d. A program to pay for college tuition for immigrants in the US

Find Further Information

本文に基づいて、朝食メニューへのハワード・シュルツの要求と、それに対するマネジメントチームの対応について答えましょう。

1. Schultz's demand for the breakfast menu

   _____

2. The management team's response to Schultz's demand

   _____

Dictation & Conversation Practice ⊙ CD1-69

音声を聞いて空欄を埋め、会話をペアで練習しましょう。

Two colleagues, Carla and Jack, are going to have coffee before a meeting.

Carla: Jack, we have two hours to kill. ^{1.}_____
_____?

Jack: Sure. I think the next meeting is going to be long, so coffee is what I need.

Carla: There's a Starbucks right around the corner. Is that okay?

Jack: Okay, but ^{2.}_____. There is always a long line of people.

Carla: In that case, we could go to another coffee shop or café. There are lots of them around here.

Jack: ^{3.}_____, but I don't want any people smoking in the coffee shop. Some Japanese coffee shops have smoking sections.

Carla: That's true. Then how about going to another Starbucks? It's not far from here. We can get there in 10 minutes or so.

Jack: That's not bad at all. ^{4.}_____. Let's go there, then. Starbucks has good coffee and other nice drinks. It's also comfortable.

Carla: That sounds good. I'll get my morning cappuccino.

Jack: Okay, let's go get a coffee and ^{5.}_____
_____.

What Do You Think...? ▶次のトピックについて、クラスメートと話し合いましょう。

1. Discuss what you like about Starbucks as well as what you think should be improved (e.g. drinks, snacks, facilities, service, price, interior design, etc.).
2. The article lists five lessons that people can learn from Howard Schultz. Add one more lesson to the list. Explain what your lesson #6 would be.

07

"It was easy to see McDonald's as being on the wrong side of history."

McDonald's Modern Marketing Methods
顧客に寄り添う新たなマーケティング戦略

McDonald's はグローバルに展開するファストフードチェーンで、全世界における店舗数は3万5千店を超えると言われている。低価格の商品は学生や子供連れの家族にも人気で、車で簡単にアクセスできるドライブスルーも売上に貢献している。しかし、食の安全性の問題などが浮上し、McDonald's のハンバーガーの人気に陰りが出てきた。新たに着任した最高経営責任者は、どのような姿勢と戦略でこの危機を乗り切ったのであろうか。

Before You Read

トピックに関する次の質問に答えましょう。

1. Do you eat at McDonald's? If you do, what do you usually order?
2. What other fast food restaurants do you like to eat at? What do you like about them?

Vocabulary

単語の日本語訳を選択肢より選び、その記号を記入しましょう。余分な選択肢が2つあります。

1. disparage   (   )   6. bombard   (   )
2. critic   (   )   7. unfold   (   )
3. progressive   (   )   8. tweet   (   )
4. pronouncement   (   )   9. assure   (   )
5. pledge   (   )   10. coincidence   (   )

a. 誹謗・軽蔑する	d. 説得する	g. 擁護者	j. 批評家
b. 誓う、約束する	e. 保証する、安心させる	h. 偶然の一致	k. つぶやき
c. 進歩的な	f. 広がる、展開する	i. 浴びせる	l. 意見表明、発表

Read the Article

[1] Last year was a tough one for many of the world's biggest brands. But, as the new year arrived, one member of the US corporate elite was demonstrating that it is possible for a well-known — and frequently disparaged — brand name to regain its marketing mojo in fairly short order.

[2] McDonald's is on a stock market roll, months after it appeared to be the Fortune 500 equivalent of toast. Shares in the restaurant chain have rallied by roughly a third since their lows in January 2015, when the company named Steve Easterbrook to replace Don Thompson as chief executive. McDonald's same-store sales in the US rose — 0.9 percent — in the third quarter for the first time in a couple of years.

[3] When Mr. Easterbrook, a 48-year-old native of Watford in England, grabbed the company reins, it was easy to see McDonald's as being on the wrong side of history. Younger consumers are opting for healthier food and new burger chains, such as New York celebrity chef Danny Meyer's Shake Shack, have appeared on the scene to offer consumers chopped meat that actually tastes like something that came from a cow.

[4] What fascinates me about Mr. Easterbrook is that he responded to these travails with the corporate equivalent of political correctness. He didn't argue with his company's critics or mock the millennials. He tried to engage them. Tieless and with the straightest of C-suite faces, Mr. Easterbrook appeared on video to describe McDonald's as a "modern progressive burger company" that would "be more progressive around our social purpose in order to deepen our relationships with communities on the issues that matter to them."

[5] Granted, this pronouncement was kind of vague. But so was Ronald Reagan's verdict that it was "morning in America again" or Barack Obama's "yes, we can" slogan. The key point is that as a marketer, Mr. Easterbrook opted to go with the new-age sociopolitical flow. McDonald's pledged that by 2017 its US restaurants would only use chickens that are "not raised with antibiotics important in human medicine." In Germany, it trotted out its first 100 percent organic beef burger, using meat sourced from farms that eschew synthetic chemical fertilisers and pesticides.

[6] To be sure, many of his innovations have been little more than variations on the old business axiom that holds the customer is always right. Mr. Easterbrook is giving the people what they want, such as all-day breakfast in the US, a splendid innovation in the view of this reporter, who has not willingly eaten a McDonald's burger since the days when colour television still seemed novel, but doesn't mind an Egg McMuffin or a cup of McDonald's coffee at a pinch.

7 What's new is that Mr. Easterbrook is adjusting to the new communications landscape facing even the wealthiest corporations and the most well funded politicians. Long gone are the days when leading advertisers could control their "narrative" by bombarding the public with 30-second television commercials. Instead, they have to figure out ways to join the "national conversation," as it is known in the advertising game.

8 The order of the day is to lead from behind, as it were, and jump into the dialogue unfolding on social media when it suits a marketer's purposes. A well-timed press release or tweet in this context can be just as meaningful as the most artful advertisement. Indeed, Mr. Easterbrook's "modern progressive burger company" formulation recalls one of the great marketing campaigns in McDonald's history. Devised by Keith Reinhard, most recently of the DDB advertising agency, it was meant to assure the growing number of working mothers in the US of the 1970s that it was OK to take their kids out for a fast-food meal. "You deserve a break today," went the celebrated jingle.

9 By casting himself as a progressive burger flipper, Mr. Easterbrook is also taking a page out of the playbook of one of today's most successful consumer companies: Starbucks. When it comes to corporate do-gooders, there is no one quite like its chief executive, Howard Schultz.

10 The apotheosis came last year when Mr. Schultz told his employees to write the words "race together" on beverages in the hope of stimulating conversations on US race relations. The Twitterati responded with derision, which was understandable, because sometimes people go to Starbucks for the coffee.

11 Lost in all the online snark was the fact that Mr. Schultz's share price was also climbing rapidly. His shares have been trading recently around 50 percent above their levels at the start of last year. Maybe that's just a coincidence. But maybe it's more than that. Maybe executives such as Mr. Schultz and Mr. Easterbrook are showing us all how successful capitalists behave nowadays.

(Jan. 1, 2016 Financial Times)

Notes

1. marketing mojo「マーケティングに関する超自然的力、魔力」 in fairly short order「かなり短い期間で」
2. on a stock market roll「株式市場で好調で」 equivalent of toast「破滅（深刻なトラブルに陥っている）に等しい」 rally「（株式相場などが）回復・反騰する」
3. Watford「ワトフォード。イギリスのロンドン北西部に位置し、ベッドタウンとなっている」 Shake Shack「2004年に誕生した、ニューヨークに本社を持つカジュアルレストランチェーン。クオリティの高いハンバーガー、デザート、アルコールも楽しめ、世界中に店舗を拡大」
4. millennials「ミレニアル世代。1980年代から2000年代前半に生まれた世代を指す」 C-suite「経営役員幹部レベル。役職にC (chief) がつく役員 (CEO, COO, CIO, CFOなど)」
5. verdict「意見、宣言」 sociopolitical flow「社会政治的な流れ」 antibiotics「抗生物質」 trot out「～を披露する、発表する」 organic beef「有機生産されたビーフ。有機栽培による牧草の提供はもとより、生態系のバランスを維持しながら、ストレスを与えない放牧スタイルで自然な環境のもと育成される」 fertilisers「肥料」 pesticides「殺虫剤」
6. axiom「主義、原理」 at a pinch「危急の場合、切羽詰まった時」
8. DDB (Doyle Dane Bernbach)「1949年にニューヨークで創立された広告代理店。創設者3名の姓の頭文字から命名された」 celebrated jingle「賞賛された・有名なうたい文句」
9. burger flipper「（コックとして）ファストフード（ハンバーガー）店で働く人（調理人）」 do-gooders「理想主義的な社会改良家、慈善家」
10. apotheosis「極め付き、極致」 race relations「人種間関係、異民族間関係」 Twitterati「ツイッターを頻繁に利用する人」 with derision「あざけり・軽蔑を持って」
11. snark「皮肉な批評」 capitalists「資本家、資本主義者」

Key Terms

Fortune 500
　アメリカのフォーチュン誌が年1回発行する、全米の総収益上位500社のランキングリスト。

in the third quarter
　第3四半期に。ビジネスの上では、一年を四等分した期間（3か月）を四半期と呼ぶ。会計年度が4月から始まる場合、4～6月が第1四半期、7～9月が第2四半期、10～12月が第3四半期、1～3月が第4四半期となる。

political correctness
　（言動の）政治的公正・正当性・妥当性。言葉や社会から偏見や差別をなくすこと。

Grasp the Main Points

本文の内容と合っているものにはT、異なっているものにはFを書き入れましょう。

1. McDonald's sales went down for the first time in two years after the new CEO took office. ( )
2. McDonald's faces competition from another famous burger restaurant and young consumers' preferences for healthier food. ( )
3. McDonald's new CEO criticized what critics say about McDonald's because their opinions are biased. ( )
4. In responding to customer requests, McDonald's now sells all-day breakfast around the world. ( )
5. In the past, companies mainly used TV commercials to promote their businesses, which was sufficient. ( )

Look for Specific Information

本文の内容に関して、次の選択肢問題に答えましょう。

1. What did McDonald's in Germany introduce?
   a. All-day Egg McMuffins
   b. Chickens raised without the injection of antibiotics
   c. A cup of McDonald's coffee
   d. An organic beef burger

2. What was the slogan of McDonald's in the 1970s?
   a. "Modern progressive burger company"
   b. "Yes, we can"
   c. "You deserve a break today"
   d. "Race together"

3. Besides press releases, what is considered to be as meaningful as the most artful advertisement?
   a. 30-second television commercials
   b. Dialogues with consumers, using social media
   c. Special marketing campaigns with free drinks
   d. Half-price offers to celebrate customers' birthdays

Find Further Information

本文に基づいて、McDonald's の新最高経営責任者の戦略について答えましょう。

New CEO, Steve Easterbrook's strategy

_____

Dictation & Conversation Practice

音声を聞いて空欄を埋め、会話をペアで練習しましょう。

Kenji, a Japanese student in Australia, asks his friend, Cathy, about marketing.

Kenji: Hi Cathy. I'm doing a marketing project for my class on 21st century branding. May I ask you some questions?

Cathy: Sure, Kenji. Go ahead.

Kenji: In class we're studying ¹._____
_____.

Cathy: I see. What are your questions?

Kenji: First, ²._____
_____. Why are you loyal to those particular brands?

Cathy: Let's see. I really like Down Under Coffee. Of course, they have good coffee, but ³._____.

Kenji: Why is that important to you?

Cathy: I want to spend my money at companies that ⁴._____
_____. So, I like the brands that I think are doing positive things.

Kenji: You know what? It seems that many people are very loyal to socially conscious brands, even if they are a little more expensive.

Cathy: Many of my friends feel the same way. ⁵._____
_____, it becomes easier to become loyal to that company.

What Do You Think...? ▶次のトピックについて、クラスメートと話し合いましょう。

1. What brands are you loyal to and why do you like them so much?
2. Do you think marketing campaigns can change the way people think, or are the campaigns only good for selling products? Explain your opinion.

"TED has grown into a public-facing behemoth over the past three decades."

Photo by TEDxKyoto

How TED Evolves and Where It Wants to Go Next
「広げる価値のあるアイデア」プレゼンの進化

TED (Technology Entertainment Design) カンファレンスが始まって約30年が経ち、今では世界中で多くの視聴者が TED Talks の動画を観る機会も増えてきた。さらに、TED 本部からライセンスを取得して、TED スタイルのプレゼンを行う TEDx イベントが、日本を含め世界各地で開催されている。当初は知名度の低かった TED は、どのようにして大きく進化を遂げ、世界的に知られるようになったのか、そしてこれからどのような発展を成し遂げようとしているのだろうか。

Before You Read

トピックに関する次の質問に答えましょう。

1. Have you ever watched TED talks? What are some of the TED talks you like? How do you choose the TED talks you like to watch among so many talks?
2. Have you ever participated in a TEDx event in your city or university? If yes, how did you like the event? If no, would you like to attend a TEDx event?

Vocabulary

単語の日本語訳を選択肢より選び、その記号を記入しましょう。余分な選択肢が2つあります。

1. quintessential (　)
2. paralyze (　)
3. crucial (　)
4. descend (　)
5. flub (　)
6. bestow (　)
7. migration (　)
8. engulf (　)
9. crave (　)
10. lucid (　)

a. 落ちる、低下する	d. 渇望する	g. あきらめる	j. 麻痺させる
b. 飲み込む	e. 極めて重要な	h. 明快な	k. しくじる
c. 移動、移行	f. 典型的な	i. 分析	l. 与える

Read the Article

[1] TED started 33 years ago as a low-budget, in-person series of 18-minute talks. In the past decade, it's grown into a $65 million juggernaut. All around the world, TED produces talks (available to watch online), podcasts, and books, offers fellowships and grants, and gives little-known speakers the chance to become industry leaders just by taking the TED stage.

[2] This month it's launching its most ambitious project yet, "TED Talks India: Nayi Soch," an eight-part TV series that will be broadcast in Hindi. It's TED's first non-English TV program, and it's expected to reach millions of people.

[3] TED has hit an inflection point. The company was founded on the premise that fresh, innovative ideas can shape the future. But as social-media bubbles have made it easier to ignore ideas that don't appeal to us, an increasing number of people seem uninterested in stepping out of their comfort zone. Whether it's Trump's election win or the UK's Brexit, the world has shown signs of turning inward. TED's success hinges on that not happening.

[4] TED relies on a three-pronged test to determine if a talk is worth including in a conference lineup. The first is whether the talk gives people a fresh way of seeing the world. Head of TED, Chris Anderson's quintessential example is Barry Schwartz's 2005 talk, "The Paradox of Choice," in which Schwartz, a psychologist, suggested that people can be paralyzed by how much choice they have, not liberated by it. The second is whether the talk offers the audience a clever solution to a given problem, or the promise of a better future. The third is inspiration. The talk should express an idea in a way that compels people to act.

[5] The test has come to be even more crucial over the past few years. In a press call ahead of this year's TED Conference, Anderson said that "ideas have never mattered more." "We have this tool for bridging that allows any two humans to see the world a bit differently. Call the tool what you want: reason, discussion, sharing of ideas. It's actually an amazing thing that it can happen at all," Anderson told Business Insider. "The single most terrifying thing about the current moment is that we are throwing away that superpower and descending into more animal-like behavior."

[6] When designer and architect Richard Saul Wurman launched TED in 1984, he called it the dinner party he always wanted to have but couldn't. Wurman united technology, entertainment, and design into one multiday event. He called it "TED." Wurman and his assistant organized the first TED conference for 300 of Wurman's closest friends and colleagues. If someone flubbed a line or lost their way entirely, Wurman, who sat onstage for every talk, would sometimes

leave his chair and stand directly behind the speaker. It was his quiet way of saying, "Time to wrap things up."

7 Despite TED's unveiling of the world's first compact disc — quite the feat at the time — it wasn't until 1990 that Wurman held his second conference. Gradually, the event began to attract bigger names and bigger audiences. "Steve [Jobs] would call me up at home and say, 'What stuff do you want at the conference this year as far as equipment?'" Wurman recalled.

8 Wurman sold the enterprise, in 2000, to Future PLC, a publishing company that Anderson had built into a media giant in the 1990s. Through his personal nonprofit, the Sapling Foundation, Anderson bought TED from Future PLC in 2001 for $6 million. The company has stayed under Anderson's watch since. Under Anderson's stewardship, TED has grown into a bona-fide kingmaker.

9 Anderson saw the TED acquisition as his big second chance to deliver these kinds of inventive ideas to millions, if not billions, of people. By 2006, he had broadened its scope so that religious leaders, artists, life coaches, poets, and other bright minds could join original stars like Jane Goodall and Stewart Brand on the TED stage. The son of two missionaries, Anderson also bestowed upon TED a subtitle: "ideas worth spreading." TED is now a household name in educated, urban pockets of the US and beyond.

10 Anderson's goal is to allow the 3 to 5 billion people expected to come online by 2020 to draw inspiration from TED. He called this digital migration "the most extraordinary social experiment we've seen in history."

11 As TED has grown into a public-facing behemoth over the past three decades, it's been forced to reevaluate what kinds of responsibilities it has to the people who catch wind of its ideas.

12 TED's role as global ideas curator comes with an open-ended future, and it's a matter of ongoing discussion inside the company, Colin Helms, TED's head of media said.

13 Even though the world is engulfed in a crisis of ideas, Anderson said people still crave rational, lucid insight into issues related to their basic livelihoods and ongoing challenges. He brought up the rise of artificial intelligence and wealth inequality as two examples.

(Dec. 10, 2017 *Business Insider France*)

Notes

1 juggernaut「止めることのできない巨大なもの。ここでは巨大化した組織の TED を指す」

3 an inflection point「転換点」 on the premise「〜という仮定・前提の下で」 hinge on「〜を要とする、〜次第である」

4 a three-pronged test「三部構成のテスト。TED におけるプレゼンとして、三つの要素を満たしているかを判定する」 Chris Anderson「TED の現在の代表者で、TED カンファレンスのキュレーターも務める」 "The Paradox of Choice"「『選択のパラドックス』。心理学者のバリー・シュワルツが、選択の自由という社会の根幹をなす教義について話したトークで、選択は人を自由にするのではなく無力にし、また幸せではなく不満足にさせていると説く」

6 Richard Saul Wurman「建築家でグラフィックデザイナー。特に情報デザインや情報アーキテクチャーといった情報表現技術の先駆者と称される。TED の創始者」

8 Future PLC「1985 年創立のイギリスのメディア企業。ビデオゲーム、映画、音楽などの分野で多くの雑誌を発行している。クリス・アンダーソンは 2001 年に Future PLC を離れ、その後、非営利団体 Sapling Foundation の代表として TED を買収した。なお、PLC は Public Limited Company（公開有限会社）の略で、イギリスで使われる表現」 stewardship「管理、経営」 a bona-fide kingmaker「本物の実力者」

9 Jane Goodall「イギリスの動物行動学者・人類学者で国連平和大使も務めた。TED では、"What Separates Us from Chimpanzees?" や、"How Humans and Animals Can Live Together" のタイトルでプレゼンをした」 Stewart Brand「作家・編集者・環境保護主義者。TED では、"What Squatter Cities Can Teach Us", "The Long Now", "4 Environmental 'Heresies'" などのタイトルでプレゼンをした」

11 a public-facing behemoth「一般大衆にひらかれた巨大組織（巨獣）」

Key Terms

TED

　Technology Entertainment Design の略。TED はニューヨークに本部を置く非営利団体で、毎年春に 5 日間で 100 名以上がプレゼンを行う TED カンファレンスをカナダのバンクーバーで開催。最近では、TED からライセンスを得たオーガナイザーが、日本をはじめ世界各地で独立した TEDx イベントを開催している。

Nayi Soch

　インドで放映された TED プレゼンテーションプログラム。TED にとっては新しい境地の開拓となった。

UK's Brexit

　イギリスの EU 離脱。2016 年 6 月の国民投票でイギリスは EU からの離脱を決定し、2017 年 3 月には正式な離脱通知をした。

08 How TED Evolves and Where It Wants to Go Next

Grasp the Main Points

本文の内容と合っているものには T、異なっているものには F を書き入れましょう。

1. TED allows both well-known and little-known people to give 18-minute talks if they have good ideas. ( )
2. TED has attracted those who are turning inward on social media. ( )
3. Richard Wurman organized the TED conference every year between 1984 and 1990. ( )
4. Steve Jobs offered to provide the founder of TED Conference with some equipment. ( )
5. The current head of TED expects several million people to watch TED videos online by 2020. ( )

Look for Specific Information

本文の内容に関して、次の選択肢問題に答えましょう。

1. What is one of the features of TED Talks India?
   a. It is broadcast in English.
   b. It is broadcast in Hindi.
   c. It is broadcast both in English and Hindi.
   d. It is broadcast in various languages.

2. What is the slogan of TED?
   a. The most extraordinary social experiment
   b. Ideas have never mattered more
   c. Fresh, innovative ideas can shape the future
   d. Ideas worth spreading

3. What was TED like when it first started in 1984?
   a. It was an event mainly for the organizer's friends and colleagues.
   b. It was a one-day dinner party for designers.
   c. Steve Jobs gave a talk at the first TED Conference.
   d. The founder of TED Conference, Richard Wurman, cheered for the speakers in the auditorium.

47

Find Further Information

本文に基づいて、TED カンファレンスの話を選ぶ 3 つの基準について答えましょう。

1. _____
2. _____
3. _____

Dictation & Conversation Practice

CD1-95

音声を聞いて空欄を埋め、会話をペアで練習しましょう。

Daichi, a Japanese university student, and Michelle, an exchange student from France, are talking about how to learn English.

Daichi: I really enjoy my English classes and ¹._____
_____.

Michelle: Why do you like your classes so much?

Daichi: The teacher gives us some practical topics for us to discuss. Last week we discussed what we individuals can do for some of the United Nations Sustainable Development Goals.

Michelle: That's great. ²._____,
but when lots of people do something good, big changes may happen.

Daichi: That's true. And, ³._____
_____, too.

Michelle: Learning in the class is good, but you can also do a lot on your own, too. Do you sometimes watch TED talks?

Daichi: Yes, we've watched a few in class. Do you watch the talks often?

Michelle: I usually watch a few talks a week. ⁴._____
_____ I'm interested in. I watch it and sometimes take some notes.

Daichi: Cool. I think I'll try that. It's free, right?

Michelle: Yes, it's free, interesting and not too long. And, ⁵._____
_____.

What Do You Think...? ▶次のトピックについて、クラスメートと話し合いましょう。

1. Discuss the TED talks that you liked or that inspired you to do something for yourself or for others.
2. If you had the chance to give a TED talk, what would your topic or idea be?

"It has continued to be nimble even as it has achieved enviable scale."

Why Amazon Is the World's Most Innovative Company
「最も革新的な企業」が目指す未来

E コマース事業のビジネスチャンスを予測して、90 年代にインターネット書店を立ち上げた Amazon。長期的な視野を持ち堅調な成長を続けた結果、現在では海外 10 数か国で EC サイトの運営をするようになり、扱う商品も書籍以外に多岐にわたる。独自の物流拠点を持ち、増加する貨物量への整備を行っているが、課題も浮かんできた。革新的な企業としての新たな展開も注目を集めている。

Before You Read

トピックに関する次の質問に答えましょう。

1. Have you tried online shopping before? What site do you usually use? What was the latest item you bought online?
2. Have you ever sold anything online? If you have, how was your experience? If you haven't, would you be interested in selling items on an e-commerce site in the future?

Vocabulary

単語の日本語訳を選択肢より選び、その記号を記入しましょう。余分な選択肢が 2 つあります。

1. fixate ( )
2. startup ( )
3. autonomous ( )
4. infrastructure ( )
5. proliferate ( )
6. epitomize ( )
7. tangible ( )
8. sophistication ( )
9. variable ( )
10. counteract ( )

a. 有形の、実態のある	d. (社会)基盤、設備	g. 変数	j. 執着させる
b. 対抗する、打ち消す	e. 拡大・激増する	h. 勧める	k. 昇進する
c. 洗練、精巧	f. 典型となる、象徴する	i. 自律型の	l. 新規企業

Read the Article

1 Unlike Apple, Google, and Microsoft, Amazon is not fixated on a tightly designed ecosystem of interlocking apps and services. Bezos instead emphasizes platforms that each serves its own customers in the best and fastest possible way. Just this past year, Prime Video became available in more than 200 countries and territories, following the November debut of *The Grand Tour*, Amazon's most-watched premiere ever. Twitch, the streaming video-game network that Amazon acquired in 2014, unveiled its first three original titles from its recently formed studios. Amazon invested millions in startups that will build voice-control apps for the intelligent assistant Alexa and give her thousands of new skills. The company opened two dozen new fulfillment centers, became the largest online store in India, and made its first delivery by autonomous drone in the United Kingdom.

2 Bezos's strategy of continuous evolution has allowed the company to experiment in adjacent areas — and then build them into franchises. The website that once sold only books now lets anyone set up a storefront and sell just about anything. The warehouse and logistics capabilities that Amazon built to sort, pack, and ship those books are available, for a price, to any seller. Amazon Web Services, which grew out of the company's own e-commerce infrastructure needs, has become a $13 billion business that not only powers the likes of Airbnb and Netflix, but stores your Kindle e-book library and makes it possible for Alexa to tell you whether or not you'll need an umbrella today.

3 Amazon is a singular enterprise, one that rises to the top of *Fast Company's* Most Innovative Companies list because it has continued to be nimble even as it has achieved enviable scale. To truly understand how Bezos is meshing size and agility in 2017, though, you need to look beyond sales figures ($100 billion in 2015) and the stock price (up more than 300 percent in the past five years) and consider three initiatives that drive Amazon today: Prime, the company's rapidly proliferating $99-per-year membership program; an incursion into the physical world with brick-and-mortar stores, something the company has long resisted; and a restless rethinking of logistics, epitomized by a new fulfillment center an hour outside Seattle that features high-tech robots working alongside human workers like a factory of the future.

4 Nearly all of Amazon's most recent innovations share a connection to Prime, which by some estimates accounts for 60 percent of the total dollar value of all merchandise sold on the site. Between 40 million and 50 million people in the United States use Prime, and, according to Morgan Stanley, those customers spend around $2,500 on Amazon annually, more than four times what nonmembers spend.

5 Bezos says that people have been asking him for 20 years whether he would ever open physical stores. The answer, consistently, has been no. Yet today, suddenly, Amazon has four concepts in the works.

6 Why the shift? In part it links back to Prime; retail stores offer a tangible lure for the uninitiated. But, as Bezos explains, Amazon's technological sophistication also now makes it possible for in-store shoppers to interact with its digital platforms in all-new manners.

7 The first wave of Amazon stores is somewhat traditional: More than 30 pop-up shops showcasing Amazon's electronic gadgets. The next phase: expanding the highly curated Amazon Books stores — which showcase titles with a higher-than-four-stars customer rating alongside excerpts of reviews from the website. Amazon Go is a convenience-store concept the company announced in December. After a shopper swipes a code on her mobile phone at the entryway turnstile, she can grab whatever items she likes; they are magically added to her digital cart and automatically paid for when she leaves, through her existing account. This ability to skip both the line and any cash register on the way out is made possible by Amazon's cloud computing, machine learning, voice control, and logistics know-how. Finally, and more quietly, another grocery-store concept is also being prepped.

8 Amazon's recently opened fulfillment center, in DuPont, Washington, which looks from the outside like a generic warehouse, but what's inside represents a huge advance in the way Amazon sorts, packs, and ships orders. It starts with a "vision tunnel," a conveyor belt tented by a dome full of cameras and scanners. As each box comes off the truck, it is photographed and scanned on all sides. Image-recognition algorithms then sort each parcel based on variables such as the type of product or size and weight. What takes humans with bar-code scanners an hour to accomplish at older fulfillment centers can now be done in half that time.

9 Amazon's business is not without its challenges. The company's imperative to deliver more stuff faster has ratcheted up its annual shipping costs north of $11 billion, reinforcing the pressure to wring efficiencies out of the company's processes and its people. In the run-up to last year's holiday shopping season, pilots who work for Amazon's Prime Air shipping contractors went on strike, demanding hiring increases to reduce their workload. Amazon is working to counteract this legacy. The company pledged to create more than 100,000 full-time positions over the next 18 months.

(Feb. 13, 2017 *Fast Company*)

Notes

1. **Bezos (Jeffrey Preston Bezos)**「ジェフェリー・プレストン・ベゾス。アメリカの実業家。Amazon.com の共同創設者で、CEO（最高経営責任者）でもある」 **Prime Video**「Amazon プライムビデオとは、Amazon プライム会員に登録するとプライム対象の映画やアニメ、ドラマが見放題となるサービス」 **Alexa**「2014 年に Amazon が開発し人工知能を搭載した機器で、音声指示に従い天気や交通情報、ポッドキャストなどをリアルタイムで提供する」 **fulfillment centers**「フルフィルメントセンター。顧客のニーズに対応するためのアマゾン独自の配送センター」

2. **in adjacent areas**「周辺近隣地域で」 **logistics capabilities**「物流（管理）機能、ロジスティクス機能」 **e-commerce (electronic commerce)**「電子商取引」 **Netflix**「1997 年にアメリカのカリフォルニア州に設立された、映像ストリーミングを配信する会社。動画ソフトの販売や映像コンテンツの制作も行う」

3. **nimble**「機転の利く」 **enviable scale**「誰もがうらやむ規模」 **mesh**「かみ合わせる、バランスをとる」 **an incursion into**「～への侵入」

6. **lure**「魅力、魅了するもの」 **the uninitiated**「未経験者、初心者。ここではデジタルショッピングの経験のない人の意味」

7. **curate**「収集して整理・厳選する」 **turnstile**「回転式ゲート」

8. **tented**「（テント状に）覆われた」 **algorithms**「アルゴリズム。プログラムに基づく手順、操作」

9. **imperative**「責務」 **rachet up**「～を徐々に上げる」 **north of**「（金額などが）～を超えて、～より多い、～以上」 **wring**「もぎ取る」

Key Terms

brick-and-mortar stores
　（レンガやモルタルでできた）実際に商品を売る店舗。実店舗を持たない電子商取引と対比して使われる。

pop-up shops
　ポップアップ・ショップ。期間限定で出店する店舗のこと。空き店舗などに突然出店し、一定期間で消えてしまうことからこのように呼ばれる。

cloud computing
　クラウド・コンピューティング。インターネットを経由したコンピューター資源の利用形態の一つ。ソフトウェアを持たずとも、インターネットを介して、サービスを好きな時にどこでも利用することが可能となる。

09 Why Amazon Is the World's Most Innovative Company

Grasp the Main Points

本文の内容と合っているものには T、異なっているものには F を書き入れましょう。

1. Amazon provides a platform where apps and services are interconnected like Apple, Google, and Microsoft. ( )
2. Amazon has its own team to develop its voice-control apps for the intelligent assistant Alexa. ( )
3. Amazon made its first delivery of items, using an autonomous drone in the United States. ( )
4. Amazon, which has been reluctant to open its physical stores for two decades, has finally decided to open different types of stores. ( )
5. As the pressure of providing efficient delivery service grew stronger, pilots for Amazon Prime Air went on a strike to demand more employees. ( )

Look for Specific Information

本文の内容に関して、次の選択肢問題に答えましょう。

1. What is the name of the video-game network Amazon acquired in 2014?
   a. Prime Video
   b. Alexa
   c. Twitch
   d. Netflix

2. How much more do members of Prime spend on Amazon annually than nonmembers?
   a. More than two times
   b. More than four times
   c. More than five times
   d. More than six times

3. What kind of technology makes the work of the fulfillment center easier?
   a. Bar-code scanners
   b. Voice-control machines
   c. Cloud computing
   d. Image-recognition algorithms

Find Further Information

本文に基づいて、Amazon Go のユニークな特徴について答えましょう。

1. What is Amazon Go?
   _____

2. What are the unique features of Amazon Go?
   _____

Dictation & Conversation Practice

音声を聞いて空欄を埋め、会話をペアで練習しましょう。

Maria and Yuta, both business students, are talking about Christmas shopping.

Maria: Hi Yuta. Have you started your Christmas shopping yet?

Yuta: Uh, not really. I really don't do much Christmas shopping. Do you, Maria?

Maria: Oh yeah. 1._____
_____— my family, cousins, and friends. It's fun, but I'm so busy with school.

Yuta: That's a lot of people to buy presents for. Why don't you shop online? You can do it when you have just a little free time and even between classes.

Maria: Online? 2._____. I like to go to the store, look around, and get ideas.

Yuta: Really? I prefer online because I can do it at home 3._____
_____.

Maria: But, what about the fun of Christmas shopping? Don't you miss walking around with all the decorations, the music and seeing all the people?

Yuta: 4._____. I really don't buy Christmas presents for anyone. But, if I had so many to buy, I think I would stay home and open my computer to do the shopping. It would be so much easier.

Maria: Maybe you're right. I really don't have much time this semester, so I think
5._____
_____.

Yuta: Good idea. And, you can still turn your essay in on time.

What Do You Think...? ▶次のトピックについて、クラスメートと話し合いましょう。

1. Which do you prefer, online shopping or shopping at stores? Explain why.
2. If you were opening a store, what kind of goods or services would you like to offer? What would be the name of your store?

"It has been a long journey for the group after years of underperformance and missed targets."

Sony Comes Back from the Brink
起死回生を賭けた取捨選択と新たな展望

Sony はかつて、ビデオレコーダー、カラーテレビ、8 ミリビデオ、「ウォークマン」、CD、DVD、「VAIO」パソコンなど数々の電子機器を開発し、日本が世界に誇る巨大企業となった。しかし、近年は新たな大ヒット商品に恵まれず、生命保険やエンターテイメント分野などで多角経営を図るも、営業利益の赤字が続いていた。社運を賭け、ビジネスの方向転換を行った Sony の選択と新たな展望とは。

Before You Read

トピックに関する次の質問に答えましょう。

1. What kind of Sony products do you have? How do you like them?
2. Have you played video games with Sony's PlayStation or with Microsoft's Xbox? What kind of video games do you enjoy most?

Vocabulary

単語の日本語訳を選択肢より選び、その記号を記入しましょう。余分な選択肢が2つあります。

1. restructuring (　)
2. ailing (　)
3. sprawling (　)
4. niche (　)
5. speculation (　)
6. hamper (　)
7. boon (　)
8. runaway (　)
9. breakthrough (　)
10. reincarnate (　)

a. 構造改革	d. 妨げる	g. 大躍進、突破	j. 不調の、低迷した
b. 生まれ変わらせる	e. 推測、憶測	h. 主流の	k. 圧倒的な
c. 隙間、穴場	f. 援助する	i. 無秩序に広がる	l. 恩恵、利益

Read the Article

1 Six years after reporting its biggest-ever loss, Sony is no longer a conglomerate in freefall. The Japanese group behind the Bravia TV set, the PlayStation, Beyoncé and the Spider-Man films said it was on track to set a new annual profit record — expecting to beat its previous corporate best of ¥526 billion (£3.5 billion) by 20 percent.

2 It has been a long journey for the group after years of underperformance and missed targets. But at last week's quarterly results update, the company stated that the film unit was one of the company's strongest performers and would help it beat the record profits it made in 1997-98: the year it released *Men in Black*, and when Steve Jobs had yet to release the Walkman-killing iPod.

3 Now, Sony is expected to make full-year profits of £4.2 billion. If the forecast proves correct, it will be the fruit of extensive restructuring efforts launched by Kazuo Hirai, who took over as chief executive from Sir Howard Stringer in 2012, in the wake of Sony reporting the biggest loss in its 71-year history, of more than £3 billion.

4 For years a symbol of Japan's technological prowess, Sony had paid the price for being wrong-footed by rivals quicker to invest and develop new technology, such as South Korea's Samsung in smart TVs and Apple in devices such as the iPod and iPhone.

5 "Consumer electronics went through a difficult phase when traditional [Sony] product categories like analogue TV and Walkmans were disrupted by new products with better capabilities provided by new companies that took market share," said Damian Thong, a Japan-based analyst for investment bank Macquarie. "Sony was slow to respond to these threats."

6 In stepped Hirai, who had been a major force in the success of the PlayStation game console, which remains Sony's crown jewel. The lifelong Sony employee decided to emulate Steve Jobs's strategy for turning around an ailing Apple when he rejoined the company in the late 1990s: less is more.

7 He took the axe to Sony's sprawling consumer electronics business, focusing only on areas in which it had a realistic chance of competing. It pulled out of areas such as personal computers, lithium batteries for phones and niche hard-to-justify ventures such as digital alarm clocks. As a result, products like the Bravia TV have flourished under a less distracted management.

8 "The company wanted to focus resources on producing the best possible products," says Thong. "Make a few products but make them very good. This is what Apple did in its turnaround phase."

9 While Sony's own smartphone business has continued to shrink in the face of fierce competition, Hirai cleverly moved into providing the smartphone image sensors — which help cameras focus and increase image quality — found in all mobile phones.

10 Now Apple, with its popular iPhone, is one of Sony's most valuable partners, helping drive revenues for the division from zero to £5.89 billion in a few years. Macquarie estimates Sony has captured half of the global market for this technology. With an eye on the next opportunity, Sony is upping its investment in image sensors for driverless cars.

11 Hirai's other major focus has been to keep the PlayStation juggernaut on track. Sales of the PS4 will reach 80 million units this year, and the games division, including its online PlayStation network of 70 million active users, is the single biggest contributor to Sony's revenue. This year the division will account for 24 percent of revenue. "It accounts for almost a third of profits and has outsold Microsoft's Xbox by a factor of two," said Thong.

12 Business is also looking up for Sony Pictures, which is set for its best year at the box office since 2014 thanks to films such as *Spider-Man: Homecoming* and *Blade Runner 2049*. Renewed optimism over the film unit comes only months after a $1 billion writedown, fuelling speculation that it could be sold.

13 Until recently the studio was hampered by the blockbuster-driven nature of Hollywood success: *Spider-Man* is its only global franchise, with the latest film pulling in $900 million globally. But the rise of high-end TV production has proved a boon: Sony's TV arm is a co-producer of Netflix's £100 million epic *The Crown*.

14 "In 2012, film was more than 60 percent of the film and TV division revenues; by the end of 2016 it accounted for less than half," says Richard Broughton, of Ampere Analysis, who adds that selling content to streaming businesses like Netflix and Amazon has become a key earner for Sony. Over a third of Sony's revenues are from gaming and television/film."

15 Sony Music has benefited from the rise of digital services such as Spotify and Apple Music. However, analysts said that another contributor to the division's strong performance is the runaway success of a smartphone role-playing game called Fate/Grand Order, which was developed by an arm of Sony Music.

16 Sony is now looking for its next big hit and has identified artificial intelligence as a potential breakthrough area. Hirai made a public statement of Sony's intent to continue to invest and innovate by reincarnating its cuddly Aibo robo-dog from the 1990s as a 21-century AI-infused hound.

(Nov. 4, 2017 *The Guardian*)

Notes

[4] **wrong-footed**「不意打ちを食わされた。ここでは、気づかないうちにライバル会社に先を越されたことを意味する」 **Samsung**「1938年創立の韓国の電子、機械、化学、金融、建設を網羅する複合企業」 **Apple**「1976年創立の電気機器開発・販売を行う世界的大手企業。スティーブ・ジョブズは共同設立者の一人」

[6] **crown jewel**「企業にとって収益性の高い事業、重要資産」

[7] **take the axe**「余計なものを取り除く、大幅に削減・縮小する」 **lithium batteries**「リチウム電池。リチウムを使用した化学電池。コイン型電池が最も普及している」

[9] **in the face of**「〜に直面して」

[10] **up its investment**「投資を増加する」

[11] **outsell**「より多く得る、売り上げが勝る」

[12] **box office**「チケット売り場、人気を呼ぶ興行」 **writedown**「(資産・帳簿価値の)評価切り下げ、償却」

[13] **blockbuster-driven nature**「超大作に左右される、超大作が優先される特性」 **pull in**「〜を獲得する」 ***The Crown***「イギリス女王エリザベス2世の苦悩と葛藤など、生身の姿を描いた米英合作のテレビドラマシリーズ」

[15] **Apple Music**「Appleの開発による音楽配信サービス。2015年に開始され、世界的に配信サービスを提供している」

Key Terms

conglomerate
　複合企業。事業の多角化を目的に業務内容と直接関連のない業種の企業を買収したり、吸収合併や連携したりすることにより成長する企業。

Walkman
　Sonyが1979年に販売を開始したポータブルオーディオプレイヤー。音楽を携帯し気軽に楽しむという新しい文化をもたらし、世界的な大ヒット商品となった。

AI-infused hound
　AI (Artificial Intelligence) 人工知能技術が組み込まれた犬。ソニーは2018年に、AIBOの後継としてさらに高度なAI技術を搭載したaiboを発表した。これは「飼い主」の好みや情報に基づいた動きをすると言われている。

10 Sony Comes Back from the Brink

Grasp the Main Points

本文の内容と合っているものには T、異なっているものには F を書き入れましょう。

1. Sony had the biggest loss in history several years ago, but it's on its recovery and it is expected to have a new profit record. ( )
2. For years, Sony had been slow in investing and developing new technology, compared with Samsung and Apple. ( )
3. Kazuo Hirai as a chief executive focused on personal computers, lithium batteries, and digital alarm clocks. ( )
4. Sony and Apple are competing with each other in providing smartphone image sensors. ( )
5. Sony sees the future in artificial intelligence and plans to innovate the robo-dog, Aibo, which was first created in 1990s. ( )

Look for Specific Information

本文の内容に関して、次の選択肢問題に答えましょう。

1. How many people actively use online PlayStation?
    a. 50 million people
    b. 60 million people
    c. 70 million people
    d. 80 million people

2. Where does nearly a third of Sony's profits come from?
    a. Consumer electronics
    b. Artificial intelligence
    c. Music
    d. Games

3. What was the speculation about Sony Pictures before the movie, *Spider-Man: Homecoming* became a global hit?
    a. Sony Pictures could be sold to another company.
    b. Sony Pictures would stop co-producing the TV series, *The Crown*.
    c. Sony Pictures would become a part of Sony Music.
    d. Sony Pictures would produce mainly short-videos for iPhones.

Find Further Information

本文に基づいて次の質問に答えましょう。

1. What was the strategy Apple used that Sony has decided to follow?
   _____

2. What are the products/services that Sony has decided to focus on?
   _____

Dictation & Conversation Practice CD2-28

音声を聞いて空欄を埋め、会話をペアで練習しましょう。

John and Laura, two students from Canada, are talking about robots.

John: Laura, look at that robot display over there. There are so many different kinds: home cleaners, information guides, and even a pet dog.

Laura: Look at the dog's eyes. They seem to ¹·_____
_____.

John: I guess so. I've never really thought that robots could be cute.

Laura: Well, ²·_____
and almost alive.

John: I'm not too sure if I want a robot in my home with me or not. What could it do for me?

Laura: Maybe not now, but ³·_____
_____? A cute robot pet could really help you when you're feeling lonely.

John: Do you think so? I don't think ⁴·_____
_____.

Laura: You might be surprised. AI is rapidly developing and in the next 10 or 20 years these robots are going to become more real. We may not be able to tell the difference, especially at first glance.

John: I don't know. ⁵·_____
_____ and a sense of closeness with a robot.

What Do You Think...? ▶次のトピックについて、クラスメートと話し合いましょう。

1. What do you think about Sony's personal robot, Aibo? Would you like to have one? Discuss what you think about it.
2. What kind of robots do you think could be very useful in daily life, especially in an aging society?

"Millennials say they simply have no time for this kind of work."

IKEA's New Business Move for Millennials
若者の DIY 離れと新サービスの導入

スウェーデン発祥の IKEA は、今やヨーロッパだけでなく、北米、アジア、オセアニアにも出店する世界最大の家具量販店。郊外に大規模な店舗を構え、様々なインテリアの使い方を見ることができる部屋を模したレイアウトは、家族で楽しむことができる。低価格で高品質の家具は基本的にすべて組み立て式となっているが、日曜大工の苦手な若者が増えるにつれ、IKEA も対策を練る必要が出てきた。さて、その対策とは。

Before You Read

トピックに関する次の質問に答えましょう。

1. Where do you usually buy your furniture or household appliances?
2. Have you been to IKEA? If you have, how was your experience at the store? If you haven't, what have you heard about IKEA?

Vocabulary

単語の日本語訳を選択肢より選び、その記号を記入しましょう。余分な選択肢が2つあります。

1. disassemble ( )
2. streamline ( )
3. collaborator ( )
4. justification ( )
5. incomprehensible ( )
6. gratified ( )
7. prescient ( )
8. subscription ( )
9. contempt ( )
10. outweigh ( )

a. 合理化・簡素化する	d. 分解する	g. 〜よりまさる	j. 先見の明がある
b. 満足した	e. 改造する	h. 定額制利用	k. 理解不可能な
c. 正当化	f. 尊敬	i. 協力者	l. 軽蔑

Read the Article

1 IKEA's acquisition of TaskRabbit, a "gig economy" platform for handyman work, is not just a business move: It's a cultural watershed, an admission by a company that has long been dependent on its customers' manual skills that it can no longer take them for granted.

2 The idea of selling flat-packed, disassembled furniture probably originated with French designer Jean Prouve in the 1930s. But IKEA founder Ingvar Kamprad copied it in the 1950s from the upscale Stockholm department store NK, which had a line of furniture that could be assembled at home with a set of instructions and a screwdriver. "They had no idea what kind of commercial dynamite they were sitting on," Sara Kristofferson's *Design by IKEA: A Cultural History* quoted Kamprad as saying. "IKEA was able to become the first company to develop the idea programmatically in a businesslike manner."

3 Flat packs and self-assembly certainly helped IKEA streamline its business processes, from shipping and warehousing to keeping a slim workforce. But the approach wouldn't have worked but for something known to researchers as the IKEA Effect. In a 2012 paper, Harvard Business School's Michael Norton and collaborators showed that using one's own hands to assemble a piece of furniture increases its value to a consumer. The psychological mechanism of the effect, which of course isn't limited to IKEA, is known as "effort justification." People value their own hard work; the Norton study showed it doesn't really depend on skill.

4 IKEA's genius is in that built-in effect. People will endlessly complain about incomprehensible manuals and even about relationship-wrecking arguments with their significant others during the frustrating assembly process. But most will eventually feel gratified. Calling in professionals is not just a wimp-out but a devaluation of the end product. So as IKEA expanded, it has accepted that some customers will require assembly, but it never crossed the line between channeling such work to third-party providers and doing it in-house. It wasn't a core competence because the business model was built, in part, on effort justification; in the same way, for example, some German strawberry growers have turned picking strawberries and making jam into a marketable "experience." IKEA didn't stress third-party assembly services in advertising. It even created artificial barriers for them, such as not making them available if a customer purchased online.

5 One might say IKEA's way of selling furniture was prescient: In this age of e-commerce, a growing number of startups sell self-assembly kits because they have no physical premises. But with this new age came a generation of customers in which one in seven people cannot identify a Phillips head screwdriver — the most common tool not included in the package that may be required to assemble IKEA furniture. According to the survey of 2,000 millennials, conducted for Moen by market researchers OnePoll, three in five of these young people "struggle with basic DIY tasks"; a third of young Americans rate their DIY skills as "nonexistent," and 25 percent will call in a contractor when a DIY task is too hard to complete.

6 It's similar in the U.K., the other market in which TaskRabbit currently operates and in which it ran a pre-acquisition pilot cooperation project with IKEA. A survey of 2,000 under-35s by Corgi HomePlan, a company that offers a subscription handyman service, found that 28 percent of them struggle with fitting a toilet seat. In addition to having few basic skills, millennials say they simply have no time for this kind of work. Whether that's true or their parents simply brought them up with a contempt or disregard for manual labor isn't important for the end result: More and more IKEA customers will be put off by the need to assemble the furniture, and, unless IKEA gets in on the assembly business, it will miss out on revenue that will flow to third-party firms. This calculation outweighs the importance of the IKEA Effect.

7 So, gig economy to the rescue. At least in the U.S., owning a company like TaskRabbit frees IKEA from having to hire assembly workers and pay for their benefits. The European Union is making noises about extending its generous worker protection practices to the sharing economy. Further expansion can be planned according to how the rules change. TaskRabbit's use of ad hoc contractors fits in well with IKEA's sensible, cost-cutting ways, if not with its original value proposition.

8 It's probably great that the younger generation is learning coding instead of sewing or plumbing. But it means that at some point, IKEA-owned TaskRabbit may have to turn increasingly to older people who still have the necessary skills to put together a cabinet.

(Sept. 29, 2017 Bloomberg View)

Notes

1. **TaskRabbit**「クリーニング、引越し、配達を含め依頼者のニーズに応じて様々なサービスを提供する便利屋的な企業。2008年創業で本社はサンフランシスコ」 **watershed**「転機、分岐点。ここでは IKEA が TaskRabbit を買収することで会社の方針を変えるという意味での転機」
2. **flat-packed**「平箱包装の。家具などを部品に分けて平らに梱包し、後に組み立てる状態のものを指す」 **NK (Nordiska Kompaniet)**「ノーディスカ・コンパニー。1902創立のスウェーデンの老舗デパート」
3. **Harvard Business School**「アメリカのボストンに位置するハーバード大学の経営大学院（ビジネススクール）。1908年設立」
4. **relationship-wrecking**「関係を壊すような」 **a wimp-out**「尻込み、おじけづき。ここでは組み立てができないためにプロを呼ぶこと」
5. **Moen**「アメリカのアルフレッド・モーエンの創設による蛇口や関連設備の商品ラインを扱う企業。近年、世界的にシェアが拡大している」 **OnePoll**「オンラインによる量的リサーチを専門とする市場調査企業。2002年創立で、本社はロンドン」
7. **ad hoc contractors**「単発の仕事や作業の請負人（請負業者）、単発の依頼を受けるような仕事形態」

Key Terms

gig economy
　ギグ・エコノミー。主にインターネット経由で単発または短期の仕事を非正規雇用で請け負う就業形態。また、それによって形成される経済形態。

sharing economy
　シェアリング・エコノミー、または共有経済。社会において物、サービス、場所などを多くの人々と共有して利用する仕組み。具体的には、自動車を共有するカーシェアリングや、SNS を通じて個人間の貸し借りを仲介するサービスなどがある。

value proposition
　バリュー・プロポジション。商品、価格、販売方法、対応などの点において、消費者から見て意味のある価値、または他社に比べて自社が誇れる優れた価値（価値命題）。

11 IKEA's New Business Move for Millennials

Grasp the Main Points

本文の内容と合っているものには T、異なっているものには F を書き入れましょう。

1. The IKEA founder came up with the original idea of selling self-assembly furniture in the 1930s. ( )
2. People who buy IKEA's furniture may complain about difficult manuals but most of them feel satisfied after they assemble the parts. ( )
3. IKEA made third-party assembly services available when customers bought its products online. ( )
4. IKEA's flat-packed self-assembly furniture comes with a screwdriver that is usually required when customers put parts together. ( )
5. According to a survey, more than half of those who were born in the 2000s have difficulty with DIY (Do It Yourself) work. ( )

Look for Specific Information

本文の内容に関して、次の選択肢問題に答えましょう。

1. What is "effort justification"?
   a. Self-assembly skills will increase as people practice more.
   b. People usually value things requiring effort.
   c. The hard work of self-assembly tasks will be highly valued by IKEA.
   d. People tend to value their work more as their skills improve.

2. What percent of young Americans call for professional help when a DIY task is difficult?
   a. 25 percent
   b. 28 percent
   c. 35 percent
   d. 38 percent

3. What will happen if IKEA does not get into the assembly business?
   a. More and more customers will call the customer service at IKEA.
   b. IKEA will provide workshops on how to assemble furniture for beginners.
   c. Employees will help customers pick up suitable furniture at the store.
   d. The number of customers and revenues will likely be affected in the future.

Find Further Information

本文に基づいて、IKEA Effect とは何か、また TaskRabbit の買収のメリットは何か、答えましょう。

1. What is the IKEA Effect?
   _____

2. What are the merits of IKEA's owning TaskRabbit in the United States?
   _____

Dictation & Conversation Practice

音声を聞いて空欄を埋め、会話をペアで練習しましょう。

Nancy, a British student, and Anders, a Swedish student, are talking about IKEA and its furniture.

Nancy: My room is too bare. I need some furniture and other things to make it more comfortable.

Anders: Let's go to IKEA. They have everything you need.

Nancy: Yeah, IKEA is good. I really like the style and ¹·_____ _____. But,…

Anders: But what? Like you said, good design and good prices.

Nancy: Well, I don't have any tools and ²·_____ _____. And, most IKEA furniture requires some DIY skills.

Anders: That's true. But, I just read that IKEA is now partnering with a new company that can introduce you to ³·_____ _____.

Nancy: Really? That would work. Is it expensive?

Anders: I don't know, but we can check. ⁴·_____ _____.

Nancy: Okay. First, let's look at IKEA's website, and I can choose some things. Then, I can send ⁵·_____.

Anders: Cool. Let's do it now.

What Do You Think...? ▶次のトピックについて、クラスメートと話し合いましょう。

1. What additional services would you like IKEA or other furniture stores to have?
2. What are the advantages and disadvantages of the gig economy for both temporary workers and employers?

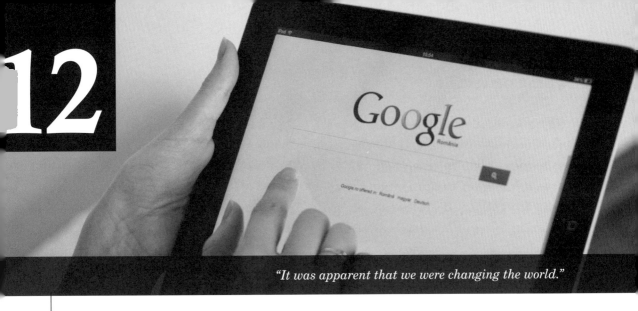

"It was apparent that we were changing the world."

How Google Has Changed the World
検索エンジンが広げた世界のゆくえ

インターネットに関連したサービスと製品を提供する Google。検索エンジンにおいては後発だったが、優れた技術開発により、世界で最も人気のある検索エンジンを生み出した。最近では「検索する」という動詞として google という単語が使われるほど身近な存在になった。企業のミッションに添い、人々が世界中の情報にアクセスできるよう日々大量のデータを整理している Google は、我々の世界をどう変えたのか。

Before You Read
トピックに関する次の質問に答えましょう。

1. When you use the Internet, what search engine do you usually use? What information have you searched for recently?
2. What kind of Google products/services do you use (e.g. Google Maps, Google Calendar, Gmail, Google docs, Google Translate, YouTube, etc.)? How do you like their products/services?

Vocabulary
単語の日本語訳を選択肢より選び、その記号を記入しましょう。余分な選択肢が２つあります。

1. milestone　　　　　(　)　　6. trivially　　(　)
2. democratize　　　　(　)　　7. robust　　　(　)
3. intervention　　　　(　)　　8. casualty　　(　)
4. retrievable　　　　　(　)　　9. curation　　(　)
5. relevant　　　　　　(　)　　10. diminution　(　)

a. 回収・検索可能な	d. 犠牲者	g. 発明	j. 関連した
b. 普通に、さりげなく	e. 理解可能な	h. 縮小	k. 介在、介入
c. 強固な、頑健な	f. 重要な段階・節目	i. 大衆化する	l. 収集、整理

Read the Article

1 It's incredible that it took just 18 years for Google — the company reached this milestone of adulthood on Sept. 27 — to create a market capitalization of more than $530 billion. It's perhaps even more amazing to recall how the search engine has changed life as we know it.

2 Google, now a unit of holding parent company Alphabet Inc., began in Larry Page and Sergey Brin's Stanford University dorm in 1998 before campus officials asked them to find a real office after the Stanford IT department complained Page and Brin's were sucking up all the university's bandwidth.

3 By the time I joined the company in November of 2001, it was apparent that we were changing the world. As an early employee at Google — the second attorney hired there — there were times when shivers ran up my spine thinking about what we were building. Democratizing access to information, and bringing the real world online — it was an inspiring place to be.

4 Having grown up in a working class neighborhood, I had to travel to an affluent neighborhood to access a good public library, spending countless Saturday afternoons with volumes of reference books to learn how to apply for financial aid to attend college. In those pre-Internet days, a good library and a kind-hearted librarian were my keys to advancement.

5 After the printing press, the first major democratization of access to information had been driven a century ago by steel baron Andrew Carnegie. He became the world's richest man in the late 19th century and then gave it all away, donating $60 million to fund 1,689 public libraries across the United States. To my mind, Google took Carnegie's vision of putting information in the hands of the general public and put it on steroids, creating a virtual library akin to those found only in sci-fi movies in 1998.

6 Google indexed the Internet extraordinarily well without human intervention, unlike previously curated outlets such as Yahoo! or LexisNexis, and in such a way that the user did not have to know how to use the index or Boolean search methods. Google enabled free searches of words or terms, making all manner of information instantly retrievable even if you did not know where it was housed. With Google, you could find any needle in any haystack at any time. Unlocking that data has indeed been a great equalizer: any individual can arm him or herself with relevant information before seeing a doctor or applying for government assistance, housing or a job.

7 Soon, Google could trivially retrieve any piece of data on the World Wide Web. Crucially, Google started indexing information that was previously offline, such as far-flung archives to make that knowledge searchable. People's photos and videos followed. Then, of course, Google cars began cruising and mapping our streets. That paired with GPS granted us all a new superpower — being able to find our way in almost any small town or big city in the world.

8 Now Google is a global archive storing our history as it is made. It is as though a virtual world is being created right alongside our real world, a simulation of reality that grows more robust by the day. Because of Google, the creation and storage of information itself has expanded exponentially as people and scholars have access to information that enables them to make new discoveries. Those discoveries, in turn, are shared with the world thanks to the culture of sharing that has been central to the Internet and Google's philosophy. All this has sped the pace of discovery.

9 Of course, there have been casualties. Google has changed the business of newspapers forever and virtually single-handedly run most publishers of maps out of business. It transformed advertising, using and perfecting A/B testing to understanding our tastes and what makes a person click on an ad. Sometimes I worry that technology companies have become almost too good at this, building upon and applying these lessons to other ways of collectively sucking us into our devices more and more.

10 This access to information without the curation of trained journalists carries other costs too, leading to an Internet rife with misinformation and untruth. Nowhere is that more evident today than in our rancorous U.S. presidential election, where it seems little value is placed on objectivity, making organizations such as factcheck.org essential reading. The growth of Google and the diminution of the role of the established media in our society at such crucial moments might cause Alexis de Tocqueville, who believed newspapers "maintain civilization," to turn in his grave.

11 One thing's for sure: With Google, the future will bring the unexpected and sometimes delightful. Autonomous cars, robots, gesture-sensing fabrics, hands-free controls, modular cell phones and reimagined cities are among the projects that lie ahead for the search giant that even as it is one of the world's largest companies, has maintained a startup culture at its offices, which now employ more than 61,000 people.

(Sept. 29, 2016 *Entrepreneur*)

Notes

1. **a market capitalization**「株価の時価総額。企業価値を評価する際に使われる指標」
2. **Alphabet Inc.**「Google Inc. の共同設立者であるラリー・ペイジおよびセルゲイ・ブリンが、2015 年に Google Inc. およびグループ企業の持株会社として設立した、アメリカの多国籍複合企業」 **suck up**「〜を吸い込む」 **bandwidth**「帯域幅。データ通信の際に一定時間内に処理できる情報量、回線容量」
3. **shivers run up my spine**「身の毛のよだつ思いがする、寒気が背筋を駆け巡る」
5. **Andrew Carnegie**「アンドリュー・カーネギー（1835-1919）。アメリカの実業家で、自ら鉄鋼会社を創業し大成功をしたことから『鋼鉄王 (steel baron)』と称された」 **put 〜 on steroids**「〜を増強する、極める」 **akin to**「〜と類似した」
6. **LexisNexis**「アメリカを本拠地とするリサーチデータベース・プロバイダー。法律、ビジネス、特許関連のオンラインデータベースを提供している」 **Boolean search methods**「ブール演算子（and, or, not など）を用いた検索方法。サーチエンジンのキーワードにこれらの演算子を用いて一度に入力することができる」 **a needle in the haystack**「干し草山の中での一本の針。見つけるのが困難なもの」
7. **far-flung archives**「広範囲に及ぶ古記録」
8. **exponentially**「急激に」
10. **rife with**「〜で満ちている」 **rancorous**「悪意のある」 **Alexis de Tocqueville**「アレクシ・ド・トクヴィル（1805-1859）。フランス人の政治家・法律家。民主政治における多数派の世論の重要性を指摘し、その世論を構築するのは新聞ではないかと提唱した」

Key Terms

A/B testing
　ＡとＢの広告のどちらが優れているか比較するウェブマーケティングの手法。二つの施策を比較検討する行為（試験）の総称。

factcheck.org
　ペンシルベニア大学のアネンバーグ・パブリックポリシーセンターを拠点に、情報公開前または情報公開後に、文書の不備や基準の順守などのファクトチェックを行う非営利組織。

startup culture
　支配する権力層がなく、オープンなコミュニケーションを通して、創造的な能力が認められる新規企業のような職場環境。

12 How Google Has Changed the World

Grasp the Main Points

本文の内容と合っているものには T、異なっているものには F を書き入れましょう。

1. When Google was founded by students at Stanford University, its IT department provided an office for them. ( )
2. As Google expands its business from search engine to other industries, it has lost a startup culture and become a giant corporation. ( )
3. Unlike other previous search engines, Google made it possible for users to search and retrieve information without knowing how to use the index. ( )
4. Google, GPS, and the publishers of maps collaboratively created the online maps so that we can find our way in almost all places in the world. ( )
5. Google made it easier for people to have access to both true and fake news written by untrained journalists. ( )

Look for Specific Information

本文の内容に関して、次の選択肢問題に答えましょう。

1. What did the CEO of a steel company, Andrew Carnegie, do as his social contribution?
    a. He became the world richest man in the 20th century.
    b. He donated money to fund public libraries in the United States.
    c. He created the first online library for the general public.
    d. He helped build a big steel company overseas.

2. What industries have been affected by Google's business model?
    a. Advertisement and newspapers
    b. Airline and tourism
    c. Medicine and welfare
    d. Science and environment

3. What are some of the new projects Google will be working on?
    a. Healthcare and 3-D medical equipment
    b. Space craft and jet engines
    c. Robots and autonomous cars
    d. Consumer electronics and retail

Find Further Information

本文に基づいて、Google の情報検索で何が可能になったか答えましょう。

Things that Google's search engine has enabled people to do
_____

Dictation & Conversation Practice   CD2-49

音声を聞いて空欄を埋め、会話をペアで練習しましょう。

Kazuki and Jodi are discussing Google products.

Kazuki: Hey Jodi. Do you use a lot of Google products?
Jodi: I sure do. The ones I most use are Google ¹·_____ _____. They've been very helpful.
Kazuki: I've never used the Translate app. Is it any good?
Jodi: It's not perfect, but it does help me to understand the basic meaning of some complicated sentences. ²·_____ _____.
Kazuki: I see. By the way, have you heard Google is developing self-driving cars?
Jodi: Yeah, it's called Waymo, right? It's like a taxi, but without the driver. That's hard to imagine. ³·_____ _____.
Kazuki: I know what you mean. I also read an article about smart garments Google is trying to make with interactive fabrics.
Jodi: ⁴·_____?
Kazuki: Threads woven in the fabrics have a touch sensor that controls the smartphones in the pocket. So by touching shirts, jackets, or jeans, you can answer the phone or control the volume levels of music.
Jodi: Oh, ⁵·_____. What an awesome idea!

What Do You Think...? ▶次のトピックについて、クラスメートと話し合いましょう。

1. Would you like to wear smart garments? If so, what kind of interactive clothes would you like to wear? If not, explain why not.
2. Discuss different ways to distinguish fake news from real news.

"Walmart's experiment holds some surprising lessons for the American economy as a whole."

How Did Walmart Get Cleaner Stores and Higher Sales?
再生を賭けた経営戦略の転換

アメリカのアーカンソー州に本部を置くメガディスカウントストアのWalmartは、商品の低価格化とコスト削減などを推進し、世界28か国に進出すると共に、売上額最大の小売企業となった。しかし、順調に見えた経営も、お膝元のアメリカで店に対する顧客や従業員のクレームが噴出し、経営戦略の転換を余儀なくされた。再生を賭けWalmartが導入した逆転の発想とは。

Before You Read

トピックに関する次の質問に答えましょう。

1. How often do you go to discount stores? Which discount stores do you like to shop at?
2. Have you been to mega discount stores, such as Walmart and Costco? If you have, what was your experience like?

Vocabulary

単語の日本語訳を選択肢より選び、その記号を記入しましょう。余分な選択肢が2つあります。

1. frown （　）
2. revolutionary （　）
3. wage （　）
4. shareholder （　）
5. acknowledge （　）
6. specialize （　）
7. diagnose （　）
8. loyalty （　）
9. predictable （　）
10. prospect （　）

a. 認める	d. 見通し	g. 忠誠（心）	j. 役員
b. 専門にする	e. 予想できる	h. 賃金	k. 革新的な
c. 診断する	f. しかめ面	i. 株主	l. 伝統的な

Read the Article

1 A couple of years ago, Walmart, which once built its entire branding around a big yellow smiley face, was creating more than its share of frowns. Shoppers were fed up. They complained of dirty bathrooms, empty shelves, endless checkout lines and impossible-to-find employees. Only 16 percent of stores were meeting the company's customer service goals. The dissatisfaction showed up where it counts. Sales at stores open at least a year fell for five straight quarters; the company's revenue fell for the first time in Walmart's 45-year run as a public company in 2015 (currency fluctuations were a big factor, too).

2 To fix it, executives came up with what, for Walmart, counted as a revolutionary idea. It is an idea that flies in the face of the prevailing ethos on Wall Street and in many executive suites the last few decades. But there is sound economic theory behind the idea. "Efficiency wages" is the term that economists use for the notion that employers who pay workers more than the going rate will get more loyal, harder-working, more productive employees in return.

3 Walmart's experiment holds some surprising lessons for the American economy as a whole. Productivity gains have been slow for years; could fatter paychecks reverse that? Demand for goods and services has remained stubbornly low ever since the 2008 economic crisis. If companies paid people more, would it bring out more shoppers — benefiting workers and shareholders alike?

4 Executives in early 2015 sketched out a plan to spend more money on increased wages and training, and offer more predictable scheduling. They refer to this plan as "the investments." The results are promising. By early 2016, the proportion of stores hitting their targeted customer-service ratings had rebounded to 75 percent. Sales are rising again. That said, the immediate impact on earnings and the company's stock price have been less rosy. The question for Walmart is ultimately whether that short-run hit makes the company a stronger competitor in the long run.

5 On the morning of Feb. 19, 2015, Walmart's 1.2 million employees across the United States gathered to watch a video feed by their chief executive. Doug McMillon, sitting in the office once occupied by the company founder Sam Walton, more or less acknowledged that Walmart had made a mistake. It had gone too far in trying to cut payroll costs to the bone.

6 What most store employees probably didn't know was that Mr. McMillon and his executive team, who had been promoted into their jobs a year earlier, were under extraordinary pressure from investors. They needed to reverse a slide in business and fight off threats in all directions — dollar discounters on the low end, Amazon online, direct competitors like Target and countless rivals specializing in one slice of Walmart's business, from grocery chains to home-improvement warehouses.

7 The company offers its millions of shoppers a simple way to make their dissatisfaction known. On the back of sales receipts is a message, "Tell us about your visit today," along with instructions to log on to a website and answer questions about the store: Was it clean? Were they able to get what they came for quickly? Were employees friendly?

8 In early 2015, the answers that poured into Walmart's global headquarters were, in a word, awful. A report by analysts at Wolfe Research in 2014 included photographs from a visit to Walmart of a sad-looking display of nearly empty bins of oranges and lemons and disorganized shelves of crackers.

9 The company had been busy raising profits by cutting labor costs. The number of employees in the United States fell by 7 percent from early 2008 to early 2013, for example, a span in which the square footage of stores rose 13 percent. Some of that reflects technological advances, like self-checkout kiosks. But when Mr. McMillon and a new team came in to reverse the slide starting in early 2014, they diagnosed the problem as having taken the cost-cutting logic too far.

10 From store managers nationwide, they heard that years of cost-cutting meant Walmart had become viewed as a last-ditch option for employment. They were under such pressure to keep labor costs low that the employees they hired showed little loyalty or career-building devotion to their jobs.

11 "We realized quickly that wages are only one part of it, that what also matters are the schedules we give people, the hours that they work, the training we give them, the opportunities you provide them," said Judith McKenna, who became chief operating officer in late 2014.

12 That is how Walmart decided to build 200 training centers to offer a clearer path for hourly employees who want to get on the higher-paying management track. And it said it would raise its hourly pay to a minimum of $10 for workers who complete a training course and raise department manager pay to $15 an hour, from $12. It said it would offer more flexible and predictable schedules to hourly workers. Walmart's pay increases got most of the attention. But the new training and prospect of better career paths for hourly staff members could be more significant in the long term.

(Oct. 15, 2016 *The New York Times*)

Notes

1. **for five straight quarters**「5 四半期連続で」 **a public company**「株式会社（一般に株の売買が公開されている会社）」
2. **the prevailing ethos**「一般的な気質、倫理観」 **executive suites**「重役室、会社の役員室」
5. **a video feed**「配信動画」 **cut payroll costs to the bone**「人件費をぎりぎりまで切り詰める」
6. **reverse a slide**「（売り上げなどの）下落を好転させる」
9. **the square footage of stores**「店の専有面積（平方フィート）」
11. **chief operating officer**「最高執行責任者（COO と略される）。会社の経営方針に基づいて実際の企業活動の執行にあたる役員」

Key Terms

dollar discounters
　　1 ドル・ショップのようなディスカウントストア。仕入れやコストの効率化により低価格販売を実現した小売店。

Amazon
　　アメリカに本拠を構えるウェブサービス会社。インターネット上の商取引分野の先駆者。

Target
　　アメリカで最大の売上高を競う小売業者である Target Corporation が運営するディスカウントチェーン。

13 How Did Walmart Get Cleaner Stores and Higher Sales?

Grasp the Main Points

本文の内容と合っているものには T、異なっているものには F を書き入れましょう。

1. The customer dissatisfaction with Walmart was high and the company's revenues fell for the first time in 2015. ( )
2. Since the 2008 financial crisis, consumer demand for goods and services has drastically increased in the retail industry. ( )
3. Walmart's customer service ratings continued to fall until late 2016. ( )
4. Walmart reduced the number of employees and cut labor costs from 2008 to 2013. ( )
5. Walmart employees were loyal and devoted themselves to their jobs before the current chief executive took office. ( )

Look for Specific Information

本文の内容に関して、次の選択肢問題に答えましょう。

1. What is one of the main mistakes Walmart made?
    a. They introduced self-checkout kiosks.
    b. They did not give surveys to the customers early enough.
    c. They did not pay their employees enough money.
    d. The CEO sent a message to their employees, but he didn't visit the stores.

2. What are the threats to Walmart besides their competitive mega retail stores?
    a. Mega warehouses and customers
    b. Investors and the government regulations
    c. Discount stores and online shopping sites
    d. Store managers and employees

3. What improvement has Walmart made for their employees?
    a. Wage increases, options to work from home, and more vacations
    b. Wage increases, job training, and predictable scheduling
    c. Flexible scheduling, on-sight childcare, and scholarships for college
    d. Healthcare, paid vacations, and training gyms

Find Further Information

本文に基づいて、能率賃金（efficiency wages）とは何か答えましょう。

The theory of "efficiency wages"
_____
_____

Dictation & Conversation Practice　　　CD2-62

音声を聞いて空欄を埋め、会話をペアで練習しましょう。

Two university students, Jen and Paul are talking about summer part-time jobs.

Jen: I'm hoping to get a good part-time job. Paul, [1]._____
_____?

Paul: Well, what kind of work do you want to do? Do you want to work in a restaurant, summer camp, or maybe retail?

Jen: [2]._____, but I need a place that is flexible because I'm taking some summer school classes at the university.

Paul: You know what? I just heard that Walmart is offering [3]._____
_____.

Jen: Really? Walmart? I've never even thought about working there. But, I like the idea of flexible hours and higher pay.

Paul: You should consider it. [4]._____
_____, and they are a big retail store selling everything from groceries to camping supplies.

Jen: [5]._____.
Maybe I could get a job working in the camping department.

Paul: Sure. Why not? You should really go there and apply.

Jen: I think you're right. I'll do that.

What Do You Think...?　▶次のトピックについて、クラスメートと話し合いましょう。

1. Do you have a part-time job? If you do, what do you do? How did you find the job? How much do you get paid per hour? Do you have any complaints about your working conditions?
2. Discuss ways to improve employee motivation at work, besides the increase of their wages or salaries.

14

"The streaming boom is only beginning."

Imagechina / 時事通信フォト

With Disney's Move to Streaming, a New Era Begins
映像配信サービス新時代の到来

「ミッキーマウス」の生みの親であるウォルト・ディズニーとロイ・ディズニー兄弟の設立した The Walt Disney Company。国際的な企業へと発展し、数々の有名なディズニー映画やキャラクターを生み出し、アメリカ、日本、フランス、香港、中国でディズニー・パークを展開する。そのディズニーが時流に乗り開始する映像配信サービスは、エンターテイメント業界における新しい時代の到来を告げる。

Before You Read

トピックに関する次の質問に答えましょう。

1. Do you have any Disney shows or movies that you like? If you do, what are they?
2. Have you ever been to Disneyland? If you have, how was your experience? If you haven't, would you like to go there in the future?

Vocabulary

単語の日本語訳を選択肢より選び、その記号を記入しましょう。余分な選択肢が2つあります。

1. cling ( )
2. plunge ( )
3. intensify ( )
4. overwhelmed ( )
5. underwhelmed ( )
6. accelerate ( )
7. exclusively ( )
8. deal ( )
9. substantial ( )
10. irrelevant ( )

a. 強化・激化する	d. 排他・独占的に	g. 採用する	j. 執着する
b. 加速する	e. 取引、協定	h. 相当、実質的な	k. 圧倒された
c. 無関係な、重要でない	f. 影響力のある	i. 飛び込むこと	l. 失望した

Read the Article

[1] Disney set off a sonic boom in Hollywood by unveiling plans to start two Netflix-style services: For the first time in the streaming age, the world's largest media company had decided that embracing a new business model was more important than clinging to its existing one.

[2] Disney's decision to better align itself with consumer trends instantly reverberated through the entertainment industry. Disney's cable channels, which include ESPN, have long been seen as the reason many viewers were refraining from cutting the cord entirely. If Disney was going all in on streaming, the impact would be felt by almost every television company and cable operator.

[3] Disney said that it would spend heavily on original programming for its entertainment streaming service and pull future Disney and Pixar movies from Netflix. That sent Netflix shares downward. The question seemed to be, how would Netflix, even with its head start in terms of audience and reach, manage without the mighty mouse? And would Disney's plunge into streaming encourage the likes of Discovery and Viacom to do the same, intensifying competition?

[4] And would viewers who want to eschew traditional cable subscriptions eventually find themselves overwhelmed by the sheer number of streaming services they would need to cobble together to watch what they wanted to watch? Disney investors may also be worried about the enormous spending it will take to build two streaming services. Some might have been underwhelmed by the company's plans or might have thought that the decision came much too late. While a few ardent Disney critics held that view, most analysts applauded the company's move.

[5] Disney's streaming plans call for the introduction early next year of a subscription service to be built around ESPN's sports programming. It will be powered by BamTech, a technology company that handles direct-to-consumer video for baseball teams and HBO, among others. Disney paid $1 billion a year ago for a 33 percent stake in BamTech. Robert A. Iger, Disney's chief executive, announced that Disney had accelerated an option to spend $1.58 billion for an additional 42 percent share.

[6] But this still-unnamed subscription service is designed to protect the cable bundle, at least initially. The service will offer only sports programming that is not available on ESPN's traditional channels. Only people who also pay to receive ESPN the old-fashioned way (via a cable or satellite hookup) will be able to stream ESPN's core offerings, including N.F.L. and N.B.A. games.

[7] Mr. Iger has also made an important calculation that Disney — unlike most of its competitors — has programming

that is must-have in the old model (cable and satellite) and in the new (streaming). Put another way, Disney has the power to introduce streaming offerings around ESPN, Pixar films and Disney Channel shows without worrying about being dropped by third-party distributors, including upstarts like Sling TV and PlayStation Vue.

8 Children's programming, an obvious strength for Disney, has proved especially important for streaming services. Amazon last year acquired a significant amount of PBS's library of original series to exclusively stream on its service, and Netflix has said it expects to have 75 original children's programs by the end of next year.

9 Disney's announcement had an immediate impact on Netflix, as the news media raced to pit the two companies against each other, and some investors worried about Disney taking back its movies. (Starting in late 2019, new-release Disney and Pixar films will move to Disney's entertainment-focused streaming service.)

10 Disney has not yet decided whether to pull its Marvel or *Star Wars* movies from Netflix. Netflix will not lose access to Marvel-branded television shows like *The Defenders* because Netflix is a co-producer of them. Executives at Disney and Netflix declined to comment publicly on Wednesday. In a statement on Tuesday, Netflix said, "We continue to do business with the Walt Disney Company on many fronts, including our ongoing deal with Marvel TV."

11 Notably, Netflix has been building up a huge original movie operation, including spending on the $90 million *Bright*, a forthcoming Will Smith movie. Netflix plans to start making as many as 50 of its own movies annually. BamTech, which Disney plans to use as the backbone of its streaming services, has substantial operations. But Disney faces a steep learning curve. By the time Disney even introduces its entertainment-based service in 2019, Netflix will have about 64 million subscribers in the United States and 158 million worldwide, according to BTIG Research.

12 Disney would probably contend that Netflix's head start is irrelevant. "It's high time we got in this business," Mr. Iger told analysts on a conference call. "The profitability, the revenue-generating capability of this initiative is substantially greater than the business models we're currently being served by." In the end, there was only one aspect of Disney's move that everyone seemed to agree on: The streaming boom is only beginning.

13 Netflix, Amazon, HBO Now, CBS All Access and Hulu (part-owned by Disney) are all barreling ahead online. FX is dipping a toe in the water with Comcast. AMC has done the same. And now comes Disney with two services, which will undoubtedly prod other entertainment giants to move beyond niche direct-to-consumer offerings.

(Aug. 9, 2017 The New York Times)

Notes

1. **a sonic boom**「ソニックブーム。音速以上で飛行するジェット機などの作った衝撃波が地表に達して起こす爆発音。ここでは業界に衝撃を与えたことの比喩」
2. **align itself with**「〜と同列に立つ、（消費者のトレンド）に合わせる」 **reverberate**「響き渡る」
3. **Viacom**「MTVなどケーブルテレビ局向け事業を展開するメディア複合企業。パラマウント映画を傘下に持つ」
4. **cobble together**「〜をつぎはぎして整理する」 **ardent**「熱心な、熱狂的な」
5. **direct-to-consumer**「直販の（直接販売の）」 **HBO (Home Box Office)**「アメリカの衛星およびケーブルテレビ放送局」
6. **still-unnamed**「まだ定着していない、無名の」 **the cable bundle**「ケーブル束。ここではケーブルテレビのコンテンツを指す」 **N.F.L. (National Football League)**「アメリカで最上位の人気を誇るプロアメリカンフットボールチームの加盟するリーグ。北米4大プロスポーツリーグの一つ」 **N.B.A. (National Basketball Association)**「北米で展開する男子プロバスケットボールリーグ。北米4大プロスポーツリーグの一つ」
7. **upstarts**「急に成長を遂げた企業」 **Sling TV**「アメリカのコロラド州にあるインターネットテレビ会社」 **PlayStation Vue**「ソニー・ネットワークエンタテインメントが開始した、クラウド型ライブテレビサービス」
8. **PBS (Public Broadcasting Service)**「アメリカの公共放送サービス。主に教育番組を放送する」
9. **pit**「闘わせる」
10. **on many fronts**「多くの面において」
11. **notably**「注目すべきは」 **a steep learning curve**「険しい成長曲線」 **BTIG Research**「世界中で約3,000の法人を対象に、ビジネス分析や戦略のコンサルティング、資金運用サービスなどを行っている会社」
12. **head start**「有利かつ好調な滑り出し」
13. **barrel ahead**「疾走する」 **dip a toe in the water**「（新しいことなどを）慎重に始める」 **prod**「刺激する」

Key Terms

ESPN (Entertainment and Sports Programming Network)
　ディズニー傘下のスポーツ専門チャンネル。衛星およびケーブルテレビでチャンネルを提供。

streaming services
　映像配信サービス。音声や動画など、ファイルをダウンロードしながら同時に再生することができるサービス。

Pixar
　ピクサー・アニメーション・スタジオ。アメリカのアニメーション制作会社。現在は、ウォルト・ディズニー・カンパニー傘下。

14 With Disney's Move to Streaming, a New Era Begins

Grasp the Main Points

本文の内容と合っているものにはT、異なっているものにはFを書き入れましょう。

1. One of the reasons why customers subscribe to Disney's cable channels is it offers ESPN sports programs. (　)
2. Disney is going to provide more Disney and Pixar movies to Netflix, which has a large number of subscribers worldwide. (　)
3. While investors are concerned about Disney's big spending on the new services, most analysts welcomed the company's decision. (　)
4. Disney's new streaming service will have a big impact on Netflix since Disney will immediately withdraw several famous movies, such as *Star Wars* from Netflix. (　)
5. Netflix has started to produce its own movies and will continue to do so every year. (　)

Look for Specific Information

本文の内容に関して、次の選択肢問題に答えましょう。

1. How is Disney's new subscription service designed to protect the sports cable channel, ESPN?
   a. It will only offer N.F.L. football and N.B.A. basketball games.
   b. It will only offer Disney Channel shows and Pixar films.
   c. It will provide sports programs that are not available on ESPN's traditional channels.
   d. It will provide entertainment programs that are not available on ESPN's website.

2. Which company will provide streaming services for Disney?
   a. Discovery
   b. BamTech
   c. Comcast
   d. CBS All Access

3. According to BTIG Research, how many people will have subscribed to Netflix in the US by 2019?
   a. 64 million people
   b. 75 million people
   c. 90 million people
   d. 158 million people

83

Find Further Information

本文に基づいて、Amazon と Netflix が Disney の子供向け番組と競うために、何を行っているか答えましょう。

1. Amazon

   _____

2. Netflix

   _____

Dictation & Conversation Practice　　CD2-76

音声を聞いて空欄を埋め、会話をペアで練習しましょう。

Julie and her friend Satoshi, an exchange student, talk about their plans for the day.

Julie: Satoshi, 1._____. What do you want to do?

Satoshi: I don't know, it's rainy and cold outside. How about a movie?

Julie: That sounds good. 2._____. I'll google the schedule.

Satoshi: Okay. I really like Disney. Maybe there is a Disney movie playing.

Julie: Actually, 3._____
_____. We have the new Disney streaming service. My parents signed up for it last week.

Satoshi: Disney has a streaming service? Wow, that's cool. In Japan, we have other services, but not Disney. What's on the service?

Julie: Everything. You can choose from anime, TV shows, concerts, and movies.

Satoshi: It's all Disney on demand. 4._____
_____, then. We can just stay here, stay warm, and watch Disney on the TV.

Julie: That's right. So how about we start with some Disney TV and then later watch a movie?

Satoshi: Sounds perfect. 5._____
_____.

What Do You Think...?　▶次のトピックについて、クラスメートと話し合いましょう。

1. Which do you prefer, watching movies in the theater, watching movie videos/DVDs rented at a shop, or watching streamlined movies on TV at home?

2. Disney is creating its own streaming service. What kind of programs would you like to watch on demand at home? What kind of impact do you think streaming services have on traditional media?

"The company had long taught its young executives that they could manage anything."

AFP ＝時事

How GE Went from American Icon to Astonishing Mess
栄光と転落、暗中模索が続く巨大企業

GE（ゼネラル・エレクトリック）は、発明王として知られるトーマス・エジソンが共同創業。世界的に事業を展開する巨大複合企業で、数々の日本企業との合弁会社も作り、多角経営を行っている。歴代 CEO の一人、ジャック・ウェルチはその経営手腕から、「20 世紀最高の経営者」と賞賛された。しかし、時代の波と共に経営に陰りが見え始めた GE は今、新体制のもと、会社の存続をかけて新たな方向性を模索している。

Before You Read

トピックに関する次の質問に答えましょう。

1. Have you heard of GE (General Electric)? Have you seen any electric appliances made by GE?
2. Do you have leaders you like or respect in business, politics, sports, education, or other fields? If you do, explain why you like or respect them.

Vocabulary

単語の日本語訳を選択肢より選び、その記号を記入しましょう。余分な選択肢が 2 つあります。

1. collapse   (   )   6. hone   (   )
2. dominant   (   )   7. swell   (   )
3. personnel   (   )   8. embark   (   )
4. retreat   (   )   9. unprecedented (   )
5. successor   (   )   10. contract   (   )

a. 静養する、引きこもる	d. 縮小する	g. 乗り出す	j. 崩壊させる
b. 主要な、支配的な	e. 増える、膨れる	h. 増強する	k. 個人的な
c. 磨きをかける	f. 前例のない	i. 後継者	l. 人事（部）

85

Read the Article

1 In the century following the Civil War, a handful of technologies revolutionized daily existence. The lightbulb extended the day, electric appliances eased domestic drudgery, and power stations made them all run. The jet engine collapsed distance, as, in other ways, did radio and television. X-ray machines allowed doctors to peer inside the body, vacuum tubes became the brains of early computers, and industrial plastics found their way into everything. All those technologies were either invented or commercialized by General Electric Co.

2 Unlike General Motors Co., Boeing Co., and other American manufacturing icons, GE isn't associated in the public imagination with just one industry or one product, but rather with industrial innovation itself. Famously co-founded by Thomas Edison, GE was actually run in its early years by another co-founder, Charles Coffin.

3 Since Coffin, GE's secret weapon — and in a way its dominant product — has been its managers. The company brought organizational rigor to the process of scientific discovery, and scientific rigor to management. In the postwar years, GE hired psychologists for a personnel research department. It also bought an estate on the Hudson River and turned it into the world's most famous management training center. Crotonville was a place where current and future leaders would retreat to be taught, tested, and imbued with the company's values. GE's courtly CEO and chairman in the 1970s, Reginald Jones, was the most admired business executive of his era.

4 Jones's successor was a chemical engineer named John Welch Jr. You may know him as Jack. Under Welch, GE came to be seen as a factory for elite corporate talent. The new boss placed a premium on leadership development and the ruthless culling of underperforming employees. He became the highest-profile evangelist for Six Sigma, a management philosophy based on the systematic pursuit of otherworldly flawlessness. Promising young executives were moved between distant poles of the GE empire — from medical devices to locomotives to NBC (GE bought the television network in 1986) — so they could inject fresh ideas and test themselves. Armed with Six Sigma, inspired by Jack, and honed by the breakout sessions at Crotonville, GE's organizational officer corps could run anything, the thinking went.

5 Under Welch, GE's net income swelled from $1.65 billion in 1981 to $12.7 billion in 2000, even as its workforce shrank from 404,000 to 313,000. But over time, less and less of that income came from technological innovations or manufacturing prowess or even the productivity gains Welch had wrung out early in his tenure. Instead it came from GE's financial-services arm. GE Capital had ballooned into a behemoth, giving

GE a share of the action during a period when the financial sector was the fastest-growing part of a fast-growing U.S. economy.

6 The risks became clear only under Jeffrey Immelt, who took over the company in the wake of the dot-com bubble and right before the attacks of Sept. 11. As the years went on and GE's stock price fell to a third of its Welch-era peak, Immelt came under pressure from Wall Street to do something. He embarked on a series of splashy acquisitions, for example paying $5.5 billion for the entertainment assets of Vivendi Universal and $9.5 billion for the British medical imaging company Amersham.

7 Immelt also publicly pledged to return GE to its industrial roots (with a new concern for environmental impact) and reversed the deep cuts Welch had made to research and development. Still, under Immelt only GE Capital grew. Its profits quadrupled as it gobbled up credit card companies, subprime lenders, and commercial real estate. These weren't businesses GE had much experience in, but the company had long taught its young executives that they could manage anything.

8 The 2008 financial crisis revealed this not to be the case. In the first quarter of that year, GE's profits fell short of analyst expectations by a then-unprecedented $700 million. In the decade after that harrowing experience, GE Capital was severely downsized. But elsewhere, Immelt kept on acquiring, spending $10 billion for the power business of French company Alstom. With that deal, GE had made a massive investment in natural gas power plants just as the market for them was contracting.

9 A problem in one business is exactly the sort of thing that a premium global conglomerate should be able to shrug off. Instead, the opposite is happening, with robust GE businesses being dragged down by stressed ones.

10 GE's new CEO, John Flannery has a reputation at GE as a fix-it man. Flannery is moving decisively to address the problems he inherited. He has replaced the leadership of GE Power and announced that GE Digital will be scaled back. He has also indicated that the company will forgo big acquisitions. The message is that the company, even if it isn't broken up entirely, will get smaller and simpler.

11 If all goes well, GE will become a more mundane brand. It will be less about spreading the gospel of innovation, managerial excellence, or digital disruption and more about making really good jet engines, gas turbines, and medical equipment, selling as many units as possible, and upselling clients on software and maintenance plans.

(Feb. 1, 2018 *Bloomberg Businessweek*)

Notes

1. **the Civil War**「奴隷制度存続を主張するアメリカ南部 11 州（アメリカ連合国）と奴隷解放を主張する北部 23 州（アメリカ合衆国）が 1861 年から 1865 年に戦った南北戦争」 **domestic drudgery**「家庭における骨折り仕事」 **vacuum tubes**「真空管」
2. **General Motors Co.**「アメリカのミシガン州デトロイトに本社を置く自動車メーカー。1908 年創立で、1950 年代から 60 年代にかけては世界最大の自動車メーカーとして繁栄した」 **Boeing Co.**「アメリカのイリノイ州シカゴに本社を置く世界最大の航空宇宙機器開発製造会社。旅客機のみならず軍用機、ミサイル、宇宙機器の開発製造も行う。1934 年創立」
3. **organizational rigor**「組織的な強み」 **courtly**「教養のある、洗練された」
4. **the ruthless culling**「無慈悲な摘み取り。ここでは従業員の解雇を指す」 **evangelist**「伝道者、唱道者」 **NBC**「NBC は ABC や CBS と肩を並べるアメリカの三大ネットワークの一つと言われるテレビ局。ニューヨークのロックフェラー・センター内にスタジオを持つ」 **the breakout sessions**「分科会セッション」 **organizational officer corps**「組織役員軍団」
5. **wring out**「～を絞り出す」 **tenure**「在職期間」
6. **in the wake of**「～の結果として」 **Vivendi Universal**「フランスでメディア事業に特化した会社として 2000 年に誕生。業績悪化後は、エンターテイメント部門は GE と合併し、資金援助を受けて経営は安定した」 **Amersham**「かつてのイギリスの製薬企業で診断薬や研究試薬を生産していた。現在は GE の一部門となっている」
7. **quadruple**「4 倍になる」 **gobble up**「～を吸収する」 **commercial real estate**「商業（用）不動産」
8. **harrowing**「悲惨な」
9. **shrug off**「～をやり過ごす、振り払う」 **be dragged down**「力が弱る」
11. **gospel**「信条、主義」 **upsell**「より高額な商品を売る。顧客が希望したものより上位で値段の高い商品を提案して販売したり、以前商品を購入した顧客に、より高額な上位モデルに乗り換えてもらい、客単価を上げたりすること」

Key Terms

Six Sigma

1980 年代にアメリカのモトローラが開発した品質管理および経営手法。様々な分析、管理手法を網羅して製造プロセスを分析し、それに基づいて対策を講じることによって品質およびサービスの向上をはかるというもの。

dot-com bubble

インターネットバブルとも呼ばれ、1990 年代末期から 2000 年代初頭にかけての、アメリカにおける IT 関連企業の株価の異常な高まりを指す。後にバブルは崩壊し、多くの IT 関連の失業者を生み出した。

subprime lenders

優良客・プライム層よりも下位のサブプライム層向けのローン商品貸付業者。プライムレート（優良企業に適用される最優遇貸出金利）より低い金利の貸付業者。

15 How GE Went from American Icon to Astonishing Mess

Grasp the Main Points

本文の内容と合っているものには T、異なっているものには F を書き入れましょう。

1. Like General Motors Co. and Boing Co., GE is associated with just one industry or one product. (　)
2. Psychologists worked for the human resource research department at GE in the past. (　)
3. John Welch Jr., known as Jack, placed an emphasis on leadership development. (　)
4. After Jeffrey Immelt became the chief executive of GE, its stock plunged, but he continued to acquire other companies. (　)
5. GE's new CEO, John Flannery, decided to expand the digital business with its veteran senior executives. (　)

Look for Specific Information

本文の内容に関して、次の選択肢問題に答えましょう。

1. What business section contributed to the increase of GE's net income between 1981 and 2000?
   a. Technological innovations
   b. Productivity gains
   c. Jet engines
   d. Financial services

2. In what budget area did the former CEO, John Welch, cut?
   a. Leadership development
   b. Research and development
   c. Executive management
   d. Mergers and Acquisitions

3. After the 2008 financial crisis, what industry did GE invest most in?
   a. Health care
   b. Digital technologies
   c. Natural gas power plants
   d. Clean energy

Find Further Information

本文に基づいて、GE が従事してきた事業分野や製品・サービスについてリストしましょう。

_____
_____
_____
_____
_____

Dictation & Conversation Practice

CD2-88

音声を聞いて空欄を埋め、会話をペアで練習しましょう。

Yumi and Robert are discussing the lecture they just had in their business class.

Yumi: I really enjoyed today's lecture about Jack Welch, the former CEO of General Electric. What did you think of his Six Sigma, Robert?

Robert: Yes, it was very interesting. Jack Welch [1]. _____ _____, I think.

Yumi: His Six Sigma are very popular: Critical to Quality, Defect, Process Capability, Variation, Stable Operations, and Design for Six Sigma.

Robert: Do you remember what "Defect" means in this case?

Yumi: It means [2]. _____ _____. So, it is important to analyze the reasons for business failure and try to improve them.

Robert: I see. And, I think the "Variation" sigma is vital, too. [3]. _____ _____.

Yumi: Yeah, that's essential. I think many companies have used that sigma [4] _____ _____.

Robert: I want to work for a company that customers feel attached to.

Yumi: Me too. I want to be successful and make money. But, [5]. _____ _____.

What Do You Think...? ▶次のトピックについて、クラスメートと話し合いましょう。

1. What skills do you need to improve in order to be a leader?
2. What do you think GE should do in order to turn around its business?

Word List
予習・復習用語彙リスト

- 各課より、重要語彙を 30 語ずつ選定しました。
- 太字は各課の Vocabulary で出題されている語句です。

01 Zara

- ☐ account (for)
- ☐ bankruptcy
- ☐ billionaire
- ☐ breakaway
- ☐ CEO (chief Executive Officer)
- ☐ chairman
- ☐ churn (out)
- ☐ discernible
- ☐ **divine**
- ☐ **flagship**
- ☐ generate
- ☐ hierarchy
- ☐ identical
- ☐ inventory
- ☐ **prowess**
- ☐ react (to)
- ☐ **reflect**
- ☐ **release**
- ☐ **replicate**
- ☐ **retailer**
- ☐ **revenue**
- ☐ **struggle**
- ☐ supply chain
- ☐ **surpass**
- ☐ tinker
- ☐ turnaround
- ☐ tweak
- ☐ unload
- ☐ unparalleled
- ☐ vaunted

02 Airbnb

- ☐ **accommodation**
- ☐ affordable
- ☐ **alternative**
- ☐ **aspiration**
- ☐ benign
- ☐ **breach**
- ☐ celestial
- ☐ **comply**
- ☐ comprehensive
- ☐ conciliatory
- ☐ ensure
- ☐ expand
- ☐ **evolve**
- ☐ fearsomely
- ☐ fine
- ☐ firm
- ☐ forecast
- ☐ **forgo**
- ☐ fringe
- ☐ hefty
- ☐ hospitality
- ☐ **impose**
- ☐ innovation
- ☐ **launch**
- ☐ lobby
- ☐ **pitfall**
- ☐ police
- ☐ regulation
- ☐ spook
- ☐ ultimate

03 Facebook

- ☐ **abandon**
- ☐ **acquisition**
- ☐ animated
- ☐ app
- ☐ arbiter
- ☐ augmented reality
- ☐ boundary
- ☐ distract
- ☐ ecosystem
- ☐ **emulate**
- ☐ **entice**
- ☐ **envision**
- ☐ feature
- ☐ fizzle
- ☐ **flop**
- ☐ flourish
- ☐ futuristic
- ☐ **grapple**
- ☐ household
- ☐ immersive
- ☐ interface
- ☐ **manipulate**
- ☐ muse
- ☐ **nascent**
- ☐ object
- ☐ replace
- ☐ **scrutiny**
- ☐ traction
- ☐ underpin
- ☐ virtual reality

04 Adidas

- [ ] adapt
- [ ] **adhesion**
- [ ] **attribute**
- [ ] component
- [ ] customization
- [ ] **defect**
- [ ] economy
- [ ] employ
- [ ] environmental
- [ ] **exclusive**
- [ ] **facility**
- [ ] fitting
- [ ] footwear
- [ ] glue
- [ ] **hype**
- [ ] in-house
- [ ] mold
- [ ] **negligible**
- [ ] oversee
- [ ] production
- [ ] **prototype**
- [ ] reflector
- [ ] revolution
- [ ] sole
- [ ] sourcing
- [ ] stability
- [ ] stitch
- [ ] subcontractor
- [ ] **supplier**
- [ ] **variant**

05 Toyota

- [ ] aggressively
- [ ] agility
- [ ] **allure**
- [ ] analysis
- [ ] appreciation
- [ ] **contrarian**
- [ ] **devoid**
- [ ] efficiency
- [ ] **elusive**
- [ ] enhance
- [ ] **eschew**
- [ ] estimate
- [ ] **forge**
- [ ] headquarter
- [ ] illumination
- [ ] imbue
- [ ] **indispensable**
- [ ] **ingenuity**
- [ ] inhuman
- [ ] notion
- [ ] popularize
- [ ] **quaint**
- [ ] quality
- [ ] radical
- [ ] resist
- [ ] solution
- [ ] sophisticated
- [ ] **ubiquitous**
- [ ] unveil
- [ ] updated

06 Starbucks

- [ ] **accountability**
- [ ] **acumen**
- [ ] approximately
- [ ] bungle
- [ ] **compelling**
- [ ] **compensation**
- [ ] **compromise**
- [ ] convince
- [ ] defining
- [ ] deliver
- [ ] **diversity**
- [ ] **embrace**
- [ ] employee
- [ ] epiphany
- [ ] evident
- [ ] **execution**
- [ ] foster
- [ ] health insurance
- [ ] **institute**
- [ ] medical bill
- [ ] **merge**
- [ ] micromanage
- [ ] mobility
- [ ] odd job
- [ ] operation
- [ ] relate (to)
- [ ] sales
- [ ] sibling
- [ ] uptick
- [ ] visionary

07 McDonald's

- [ ] advertisement
- [ ] advertising
- [ ] antibiotic
- [ ] **assure**
- [ ] **bombard**
- [ ] capitalist
- [ ] celebrated
- [ ] **coincidence**
- [ ] consumer
- [ ] **critic**
- [ ] demonstrate
- [ ] derision
- [ ] **disparage**
- [ ] engage
- [ ] equivalent
- [ ] fascinate
- [ ] landscape
- [ ] organic
- [ ] pesticide
- [ ] **pledge**
- [ ] **progressive**
- [ ] **pronouncement**
- [ ] reins
- [ ] share
- [ ] sociopolitical
- [ ] **tweet**
- [ ] **unfold**
- [ ] vague
- [ ] variation
- [ ] verdict

08 TED

- [ ] appeal (to)
- [ ] architect
- [ ] **bestow**
- [ ] broadcast
- [ ] conference
- [ ] **crave**
- [ ] **crucial**
- [ ] **descend**
- [ ] determine
- [ ] **engulf**
- [ ] enterprise
- [ ] experiment
- [ ] extraordinary
- [ ] **flub**
- [ ] found
- [ ] grant
- [ ] hinge (on)
- [ ] inequality
- [ ] inflection
- [ ] innovative
- [ ] inspiration
- [ ] inventive
- [ ] liberate
- [ ] livelihood
- [ ] **lucid**
- [ ] **migration**
- [ ] on the premise
- [ ] **paralyze**
- [ ] psychologist
- [ ] **quintessential**

09 Amazon

- [ ] adjacent
- [ ] advance
- [ ] algorithm
- [ ] **autonomous**
- [ ] capability
- [ ] consistently
- [ ] **counteract**
- [ ] curate
- [ ] delivery
- [ ] enviable
- [ ] **epitomize**
- [ ] **fixate**
- [ ] fulfillment
- [ ] imperative
- [ ] incursion
- [ ] **infrastructure**
- [ ] intelligent
- [ ] interlock
- [ ] logistics
- [ ] lure
- [ ] membership
- [ ] mesh
- [ ] nimble
- [ ] **proliferate**
- [ ] showcase
- [ ] **sophistication**
- [ ] **startup**
- [ ] **tangible**
- [ ] uninitiated
- [ ] **variable**

10 Sony

- [ ] ailing
- [ ] axe
- [ ] blockbuster
- [ ] **boon**
- [ ] **breakthrough**
- [ ] capture
- [ ] category
- [ ] conglomerate
- [ ] contributor
- [ ] device
- [ ] disrupt
- [ ] division
- [ ] electronics
- [ ] extensive
- [ ] **hamper**
- [ ] infuse
- [ ] investment
- [ ] justify
- [ ] **niche**
- [ ] outsell
- [ ] quarterly
- [ ] **reincarnate**
- [ ] resource
- [ ] **restructuring**
- [ ] **runaway**
- [ ] **speculation**
- [ ] **sprawling**
- [ ] (on) track
- [ ] underperformance
- [ ] venture

11 IKEA

- [ ] ad hoc
- [ ] barrier
- [ ] calculation
- [ ] **collaborator**
- [ ] competence
- [ ] **contempt**
- [ ] contractor
- [ ] **disassemble**
- [ ] disregard
- [ ] dynamite
- [ ] furniture
- [ ] gig
- [ ] **gratified**
- [ ] handyman
- [ ] **incomprehensible**
- [ ] **justification**
- [ ] millennial
- [ ] originate
- [ ] **outweigh**
- [ ] pilot
- [ ] plumbing
- [ ] premises
- [ ] **prescient**
- [ ] proposition
- [ ] provider
- [ ] rescue
- [ ] sewing
- [ ] **streamline**
- [ ] **subscription**
- [ ] upscale

12 Google

- [ ] adulthood
- [ ] advancement
- [ ] affluent
- [ ] akin (to)
- [ ] apparent
- [ ] archive
- [ ] capitalization
- [ ] **casualty**
- [ ] civilization
- [ ] **curation**
- [ ] democratization
- [ ] **democratize**
- [ ] **diminution**
- [ ] equalizer
- [ ] exponentially
- [ ] incredible
- [ ] **intervention**
- [ ] **milestone**
- [ ] neighborhood
- [ ] rancorous
- [ ] reference
- [ ] **relevant**
- [ ] **retrievable**
- [ ] retrieve
- [ ] **robust**
- [ ] searchable
- [ ] suck (up)
- [ ] transform
- [ ] **trivially**
- [ ] unlock

13 Walmart

- **acknowledge**
- devotion
- **diagnose**
- discounter
- disorganized
- dissatisfaction
- earning
- ethos
- flexible
- **frown**
- immediate
- **loyalty**
- minimum
- nationwide
- occupy
- payroll
- **predictable**
- prevailing
- productive
- promising
- proportion
- **prospect**
- receipt
- reverse
- **revolutionary**
- shareholder
- **specialize**
- stubbornly
- theory
- **wage**

14 Disney

- **accelerate**
- align
- announcement
- applaud
- ardent
- aspect
- **cling (to)**
- **deal**
- dip
- distributor
- downward
- **exclusively**
- handle
- **intensify**
- **irrelevant**
- mighty
- notably
- **overwhelmed**
- **plunge**
- prod
- profitability
- refrain (from)
- sonic
- steep
- streaming
- **substantial**
- **underwhelmed**
- undoubtedly
- unnamed
- upstart

15 General Electric

- address
- admired
- appliance
- associate (with)
- **collapse**
- commercialize
- **contract**
- **dominant**
- drag (down)
- **embark (on)**
- estate
- evangelist
- existence
- handful
- harrowing
- **hone**
- inherit
- locomotive
- managerial
- organizational
- **personnel**
- pursuit
- quadruple
- reputation
- **retreat**
- revolutionize
- shrug (off)
- **successor**
- **swell**
- **unprecedented**

Text Credit

01 "Zara's Recipe for Success: More Data, Fewer Bosses"
By Stephanie Baker. *Bloomberg Businessweek*, 23 Nov. 2016
https://www.bloomberg.com/news/articles/2016-11-23/zara-s-recipe-for-success-more-data-fewer-bosses

02 "Among Private Tech Firms, Airbnb Has Pursued a Distinct Strategy"
The Economist, 27 May 2017
http://www.economist.com/news/business/21722653-its-culture-cohesive-and-its-finances-disciplined-among-private-tech-firms-airbnb-has

03 "Mark Zuckerberg Sees Augmented Reality Ecosystem in Facebook"
By Mike Isaac. *The New York Times*, 18 Apr. 2017
https://www.nytimes.com/2017/04/18/technology/mark-zuckerberg-sees-augmented-reality-ecosystem-in-facebook.html

04 "Adidas Brings the Fast Shoe Revolution One Step Closer"
By Richard Weiss. *Bloomberg Businessweek*, 5 Oct. 2017
https://www.bloomberg.com/news/articles/2017-10-05/adidas-brings-the-fast-shoe-revolution-one-step-closer

05 "At Toyota, the Automation Is Human-Powered"
By Jeff Rothfeder, *Fast Company*, 5 Sept. 2017
https://www.fastcompany.com/40461624/how-toyota-is-putting-humans-first-in-an-era-of-increasing-automation

06 "How Starbucks CEO Transformed a Small Coffee Bean Store Into a Massively Successful Worldwide Brand"
By Carolyn Sun. *Entrepreneur*, 30 June 2016
https://www.entrepreneur.com/slideshow/275551#0

07 "Politically Correct McDonald's Is on a Roll"
By Gary Silverman. *Financial Times*, 1 Jan. 2016
https://www.ft.com/content/ed16ce80-aefd-11e5-993b-c425a3d2b65a

08 "How the Scrappy TED Conference Became a Juggernaut Worth Millions — And Where It Wants to Go Next"
By Chris Weller. *Business Insider France*, 10 Dec. 2017
http://www.businessinsider.fr/us/ted-talks-company-profile-2017-10/

09 "Why Amazon Is the World's Most Innovative Company of 2017"
By Noah Robischon. *Fast Company*, 13 Feb. 2017
https://www.fastcompany.com/3067455/why-amazon-is-the-worlds-most-innovative-company-of-2017

10 "Sony Comes Back from the Brink, and It's Not All Thanks to Spider-Man"
By Mark Sweney. *The Guardian*, 4 Nov. 2017
https://www.theguardian.com/technology/2017/nov/04/sony-record-profits-spider-man-playstation-crown

11 "No Phillips Head? No Problem, Says IKEA"
By Leonid Bershidsky. *Bloomberg View*, 29 Sept. 2017
https://www.bloomberg.com/view/articles/2017-09-29/no-phillips-head-no-problem-says-ikea

12 "How Google Has Changed the World"
By Miriam Rivera. *Entrepreneur*, 29 Sept. 2016
https://www.entrepreneur.com/article/283085

13 "How Did Walmart Get Cleaner Stores and Higher Sales? It Paid Its People More"
By Neil Irwin. *The New York Times*, 15 Oct. 2016
https://www.nytimes.com/2016/10/16/upshot/how-did-walmart-get-cleaner-stores-and-higher-sales-it-paid-its-people-more.html

14 "With Disney's Move to Streaming, a New Era Begins"
By Brooks Barnes. *The New York Times*, 9 Aug. 2017
https://www.nytimes.com/2017/08/09/business/media/with-disneys-move-to-streaming-a-new-era-begins.html

15 "How GE Went From American Icon to Astonishing Mess"
By Drake Bennett. *Bloomberg Businessweek*, 1 Feb. 2018
https://www.bloomberg.com/news/features/2018-02-01/how-ge-went-from-american-icon-to-astonishing-mess

---

01 04 11 15: Used with permission from Bloomberg L.P.
02: © The Economist Group Limited, London (2017).
03 13 14: The New York Times. All rights reserved. Used by permission and protected by the Copyright Laws of the United States. The printing, copying, redistribution, or retransmission of this Content without express written permission is prohibited.
05 09: Used with permission from Fast Company.
06 12: Entrepreneur Media Inc.. All rights reserved. Used by permission and protected by the Copyright Laws of the United States. The printing, copying, redistribution, or retransmission of this Content without express written permission is prohibited. Reprinted and abridged with permission.
07: Used with permission from The Financial Times. Kinseido Co., Ltd. is solely responsible for providing this abridged version of the original article and The Financial Times Limited does not accept any liability for the accuracy or quality of the abridged version.
08: Copyrighted 2017. Business Insider.
10: Used with permission from Guardian News and Media Limited.

URLS are as of 2018, April. Every effort has been made to trace the copyright holders of material used in this book. The publisher apologizes for any omissions and will be pleased to make necessary arrangements when *Challenges of Global Enterprises* is reprinted.

本書には CD（別売）があります

Challenges of Global Enterprises
海外メディアで読むグローバル企業の挑戦

2019年1月20日　初版第1刷発行
2025年2月20日　初版第12刷発行

著　者　　塩見　佳代子
　　　　　蔦田　和美
　　　　　Angus McGregor

発行者　　福　岡　正　人
発行所　　株式会社　金　星　堂
（〒101-0051）東京都千代田区神田神保町 3-21
　　　　　Tel.(03) 3263-3828（営業部）
　　　　　　　(03) 3263-3997（編集部）
　　　　　Fax(03) 3263-0716
　　　　　https://www.kinsei-do.co.jp

編集担当／西田 碧　　　　　　　　　Printed in Japan
印刷・製本所／三美印刷株式会社
本書の無断複製・複写は著作権法上での例外を除き禁じられています。本書を代行業者等の第三者に依頼してスキャンやデジタル化することは、たとえ個人や家庭内での利用であっても認められておりません。
落丁・乱丁本はお取り替えいたします。

ISBN978-4-7647-4082-2　　C1082